The Ai Accelerator

The Ai Accelerator

HOW TO 10X YOUR PRODUCTIVITY,
CLONE YOUR SMARTEST EMPLOYEES,
AND MONETIZE YOUR IP IN THE
NEW Ai-ECONOMY

MIKE KOENIGS

A Superpower Accelerator Book

Praise for *Ai Accelerator* and Mike Koenigs

"When I asked Mike to teach my Abundance360 Patrons community about Ai, I called him 'an arsonist of the mind in all the best ways.' Mike knows how to get the attention of any audience, get them engaged, see a bigger Moonshot future for themselves, and make it real with Ai. He knows how to make technology fun, engaging, and exciting for anyone who wants to live a bigger and more abundant life. **Read this book right now if you want to know how to make Ai work for you.**"

Peter H. Diamandis, MD, Founder, XPRIZE, Singularity/Abundance360
Founder & Executive Chairman, XPRIZE Foundation
Exec. Founder, Singularity University & Abundance360
New York Times Bestselling Author, Abundance, BOLD, and
The Future is Faster Than You Think

"This amazing book goes straight to the heart of the Ai Revolution, saving you a fortune in time and money by teaching you the most practical, proven methods and techniques available in this exciting industry."

Brian Tracy
Best-Selling Author, Speaker
Chairman and CEO of Brian Tracy International

"Mike combines imagination, storytelling, technology, and passion to illuminate mysteries that had previously seemed impenetrable. Time with Mike is always a delight."

Roy H. Williams
Author of the NY Times and Wall Street Journal
Bestselling Wizard of Ads Trilogy.

"For over a decade, Mike Koenigs has been my go-to guy for cutting-edge technology and marketing strategies. Every time I talk to him, he gets me thinking about new ways to use the latest tools to grow my business, reach more people, and make a bigger impact. And now, with Ai Accelerator for Entrepreneurs, he's giving you the blueprint to do the same.

In this book, Mike shows you exactly how to harness the power of artificial intelligence to automate your marketing, streamline your operations, and take your business to new heights. I was blown away by the real-world examples and practical strategies Mike shares for using Ai to create deeper audience engagement, increase efficiency, and drive growth.

But beyond just the tactics, what I love about this book is how **Mike empowers you to think differently about what's possible for your business.** He challenges you to break free from limiting beliefs, embrace change, and become the kind of visionary leader that thrives in the age of Ai.

Whether you're a doctor, health coach, or entrepreneur, you need to read this book. Mike's insights and strategies will help you work smarter, serve your clients better, and build a business that makes a real difference in the world."

JJ Virgin
4x NYTimes Best Selling Author
3x Inc 5000 Founder
CEO, Podcaster, Speaker,
Celebrity Nutrition Expert,
Fitness Hall of Famer

"I don't know how he does it, but Mike is always on the cutting edge of everything. When I want to know what's going on and how to make it real, I call Mike. He recently sat down with my husband Mike and helped him start writing his book in less than 30 minutes using Ai. It was not only mind-blowing, but it was also an emotional experience for both of us. For him to make a dream my husband had for years real in minutes, that's what I love so much about Mike; he knows how to make our biggest dreams real in minutes in a way that empowers us to do it for the rest of our lives. If you want to live in a state of abundance, read Mike's books, listen to his podcasts, and pay attention to what he's doing now—it will be the next big thing."

Allison Maslan
Pinnacle Global Network, CEO

"I'm blown away by how lucidly Mike Koenigs explains Ai and how powerfully he shows business owners how they can wield this incredible technology. Ai Accelerator for Entrepreneurs opened my eyes to opportunities I never imagined possible. This book is going to revolutionize the way entrepreneurs work and achieve their goals. Whether you want to generate a year's worth of marketing content in hours, gain game-changing customer insights, or develop new revenue streams, Ai Accelerator for Entrepreneurs gives you the tools and mindset to make it happen. I give this book my highest recommendation!"

John Assaraf
NY Times Bestselling Author
CEO NeuroGym.com

"I have had the honor of working directly with Mike on building my own accelerator program within my own industry. Working with him and his team has been a joy! **Mike has blown my mind with the nearly limitless possibilities Ai can do for my business and those I coach.** Mike has done the deep work on Ai, to levels most of us would never be willing to do, and then uses his own Superpower of taking all that information and communicating Ai strategies that you can apply in your business today. This book will transform the way you think about all things Ai and help you accelerate your financial freedom!"

Aaron Marcum
Author, Thriving Entrepreneur,
In-Home Care Industry Visionary,
Trailblazer, Investor,
Master of Applied Positive Psychology,
Keynote Speaker

"Mike Koenigs was one of the first people to give me a shot to work at Traffic Geyser in 2009, an industry creating video syndication platform. We even had one of the largest digital product launches in marketing history. He believed in me, mentored me, and started me on my journey to being of President of Kajabi. He is always on the bleeding edge of marketing and technology, seeing the future and making it real years before it becomes mainstream. So, **if you want to know what's next, do what Mike is doing. He's my compass for navigating the future."**

Jonathan JCron Cronstedt
Author of Billion Dollar Bullseye

"Mike has been my go-to online video and cutting-edge marketing guy for over 15 years. I have a technology and Ai background, but **when commercial Ai hit the ground, he showed me some things that blew me away** and inspired me to have him speak at my BiohackingConference.com event. He amazed, entertained, and inspired thousands of attendees of the world's highest-end event for biohackers. I'm working with him now to use Ai to automate our marketing and reach with 40 Years of Zen. **If you want to make Ai make sense and make it real in your life or business, reach out to Mike and his team right now."**

Dave Asprey
Author and Biohacker

The Ai Accelerator

For bulk copies of this book or general information on other products and services by Mike Koenigs, please contact VIP@PaidForLife.com.

Printed in the United States of America.

ISBN: Paperback 978-1-963911-06-0
eBook 978-1-963911-08-4
Hardbound 978-1-963911-07-7

TABLE OF CONTENTS

Foreword *1*
How to Make This Book Work for You *3*
Introduction *9*

Ch. 1 How Ai Works (The 2-Minute Guide for High-Quick Start Entrepreneurs) 19
Ch. 2 Mindset: The Trillionaire Ai Mindset™ 27
Ch. 3 Market: No Market is Immune to Ai 51
Ch. 4 Model: Simpler and Fewer Doesn't Mean Less 63
Ch. 5 Message: Create a Year's Worth of Marketing in 2 Hours 75
Ch. 6 Media: Every Language, Every Platform, Now 111
Ch. 7 Multipliers: The Trillion Dollar Opportunity 135
Ch. 8 How Ai Finally Solves the Service Trilemma And Puts More Profit In Your Pocket 153
Ch. 9 Predictions for Ai 163
Ch. 10 Your Next Steps 185

Resources *195*
Meet Mike Koenigs *233*
Book Mike Koenigs To Speak *235*

FOREWORD

By Peter H. Diamandis, MD

When I asked Mike Koenigs to teach my Abundance360 Patrons community about AI, I introduced him as "an arsonist of the mind in all the best ways." Mike has an unparalleled ability to capture an audience's attention, engage them, and expand their vision of what's possible by harnessing the power of marketing and technology.

The reality is that most people, while fascinated by artificial intelligence and its potential, are secretly fearful that it isn't a tool that they can either understand or master, and that their competition will use it to out compete them. This fear is paralyzing and stops people from engaging from even trying to play with the tech – which is exactly the wrong thing for an entrepreneur to do.

In AI Accelerator for Entrepreneurs, Mike brings his boundless energy, hard-won wisdom, and infectious optimism to the game-changing field of artificial intelligence. He demystifies AI and shows how it can be an invaluable tool for entrepreneurs and lays out a step-by-step roadmap for leveraging this incredible technology to grow your business. Mike makes it understandable, even enjoyable! He delivers just in-time, usable knowledge to provide you clarity, confidence and conviction.

As I've often mentioned, there are going to be two kinds of companies at the end of this decade (2030), those that are fully utilizing AI, and those that are out of business. It's that cut and dry.

I've seen Mike in action, and I can tell you firsthand that he knows how to make technology fun, engaging, and exciting for anyone who wants to live a bigger and more abundant life. In this book, he generously shares his proven strategies for using AI to automate key processes, generate valuable insights, and create new opportunities.

But Mike doesn't just focus on the nuts and bolts; he also challenges you to expand your mindset and embrace a more ambitious vision for your business and your life. He's a master at helping entrepreneurs think bigger, aim higher, and move faster.

If you're ready to explore AI's incredible possibilities for your business, this book is your guide. Mike's AI accelerator strategies will help you boost your productivity, connect more powerfully with your customers, and achieve your most audacious goals.

Dive into this book, implement Mike's battle-tested advice, and prepare to transform your business and future. In the age of AI, there are no limits to what you can achieve.

Peter H. Diamandis, MD
Founder & Executive Chairman, XPRIZE Foundation
Exec. Founder, Singularity University & Abundance360
New York Times Bestselling Author, Abundance, BOLD and The Future is Faster Than You Think

HOW TO MAKE THIS BOOK WORK FOR YOU

"It's going to be interesting to see how society deals with artificial intelligence, but it will definitely be cool."
— Colin Angle

I like to open up every one of my presentations by demonstrating several eye-catching, exciting uses of Ai. I say to people, "I'm not an expert. Anyone who calls themselves an Ai expert is a liar because as of right now, Ai is only about a year old."

Even though Ai has been around for a long time–it was really conceived of in the '50s, '60s, '70s–a practical, commercial version has only been around for a little over a year as I write this book in 2024.

Right now, about a thousand different Ai apps are being released every week, so it's hard to keep up with this stuff.

Instead of getting stuck in the weeds, you really need to realize that it is a tool, just like anything else. People have a tendency to overhype and over-exaggerate the importance and value of something until it settles in and becomes socially comfortable.

Having said that, I do believe, and I will to prove to you, that Ai is the most disruptive tool in the history of mankind next to fire and the Internet.

Ai is about to become what I call your first draft partner, your muse, and your rapid prototyper. That's significant because, as I'll show you in this book, you'll be able to do things in minutes that currently take most businesses days, weeks, even months.

It is a powerful capability and a huge advantage if you get started now.

Wealth and abundance are created from value extraction and arbitrage from time, labor, technology, science, knowledge, and transportation.

Unless you control a bureaucracy or a country or lead a monopoly, you're getting paid to make things better, faster, cheaper, and bigger.

Now, with Ai, anyone can amplify just about anything, whether it's a manufacturing process, the use of chemistry, chemicals, time, design, or any form of technology..

It can all be done faster.

As you read this book, I want you to ask yourself, "What would one extra hour, one extra day, or one extra week be worth to you or your business every month?"

Now multiply that across your teams, or for that matter, if you built teams of Ai "robots" who could, in fact, multiply themselves, what would that do?

Your First Draft Partner and Identity Amplifier

Today, the best use of Ai is as your first draft partner and an identity amplifier.

Let's break those down.

A first draft partner basically means that you can ask a question, solve a problem, and get a first draft done right away.

Now.

In minutes.

When I say identity amplifier, what that really means is it can make the current version of you better. Your value is a reflection of how much value you create plus the perception of you in the world. If you can improve someone's perception of you, for example, by becoming more of an expert, more of an authority, or someone who speaks with more accuracy, or you're more entertaining or charismatic, your perceived value increases.

In other words, your identity, your own perception of yourself, and other people's perceptions of you are amplified.

Your Creative Muse

Ai is also your creative muse. That means you can use this as a tool to ask questions and brainstorm. It can become your thinking partner.

You can iterate many times over and get many different points of view when you know how to speak the language of Ai.

It becomes your agent. An agent can speak on your behalf.

If you've seen the movie *Her*, the main character, Samantha, played by Scarlett Johansson, has an agent like that running around solving your problems for her. Imagine if you had a tool that could do that for you. It would be incredibly valuable.

Always working on your behalf, making you smarter, without anyone else ever knowing about it.

Think about your lawyer, someone who's keeping you out of trouble, preventing you from making dumb mistakes. In my case, I have my wife, Vivian, who does that for me all the time. I need someone protecting me (often from myself!).

Your Artist

Now, I recognize good art. I have a decent aesthetic.

But if you said, "Hey, I want you to paint something," I've never taken the time to master the tools or skills necessary.

Yet, in the past year, my ability to be an artist, to design really good-looking things in a matter of minutes... to design my own book covers, come up with first drafts, be able to create artwork that I use in my Keynote and PowerPoint presentations for speeches... I can get all of that at done at high quality in minutes.

Faster than I can make a request to a graphic designer. Faster than I can make a search on YouTube or Google. Even if I find something that works for what I need, I'd still have to find someone to make a unique original version or pay a royalty.

Those days are gone.

Ai is that agent. It's your supporter. It does what you need when you need it and how you need it.

What it Takes to Use Ai Strategically

More than anything, success with Ai comes down to your mindset, and the mindset of your team. The best approach is to bring a beginner's mind, be open, and curious.

Generalists tend to get better results than specialists. I've found that people who are specialists usually avoid areas that are uncomfortable to them.

You want to have a willingness to experiment, iterate, and do something we call "prompt stacking"–I'll show you how to do that later in the book.

Don't be afraid to to get a result, not like the result, and tell the Ai to fix it. It's perfectly happy to do what you ask again, in a new way.

The way to success author Ai is to stacking the prompts over and over and over again until you get the answer you want.

Ai is really stupid. It's really literal. And the more you learn how to be explicit and specific, the better the results you're going to get.

I like to open my presentations on Ai with some humor to get across the right mindset for Ai...

I'll put up this picture of Samuel L. Jackson and with a deepfake of his voice, which I've created just to get a reaction and to demonstrate what Ai can do, Samuel says…

"What does FAFO mean? Mike shouldn't be swearing on stage but no one told me I couldn't. Fuck Around and Find Out. You aren't going to lose a job to Ai but you will to someone using it."

As you read the book and you start to experiment with Ai, remember… FAFO.

Let's go!

INTRODUCTION

"Some people call this artificial intelligence, but the reality is this technology will enhance us. So instead of artificial intelligence, I think we'll augment our intelligence."
– Ginni Rometty, Former CEO of IBM and author of Good Power

I want you to imagine for a moment…

Imagine you are sitting in an audience watching a 14-year-old boy design a company, create a website, create a product he could deliver, and start writing a book he finished less than two weeks later that became a number one bestseller.

That's what happened at Dave Asprey's Biohacking Conference. I was speaking on Ai to an audience of 2000 founders, business owners, and entrepreneurs, probably a lot like you.

I asked the audience, "Hey, is there someone here who would love to create a business from scratch?" And, of course, I saw a lot of hands. Then, I heard Dave scream from off stage, "Pick Alan, pick Alan." Alan is Dave's 14-year-old son.

So I brought Alan on stage to do what I often call an "Ai razzle-dazzle magic trick." I started by asking Alan some simple questions like:

"What kind of business do you want to create?

He said, "I want to create a business with gaming PCs."

I said, "OK, that's going to be a really competitive market. How are you going to make that unique?"

He said, "I want to make PCs with 3D printed-head cases."

That's pretty interesting.

I asked, "How are we going to get the word out?"

He said, "I'm not sure."

I suggested, "Let's write a book."

But Alan didn't know how to write a book, so I told him, "I'll show you how we can write the first part of a book in less than 10 minutes." Using one of the Ai tools I'll show you later in the book, plus a simple prompt, we wrote the first two chapters in 8 minutes and 24 seconds.

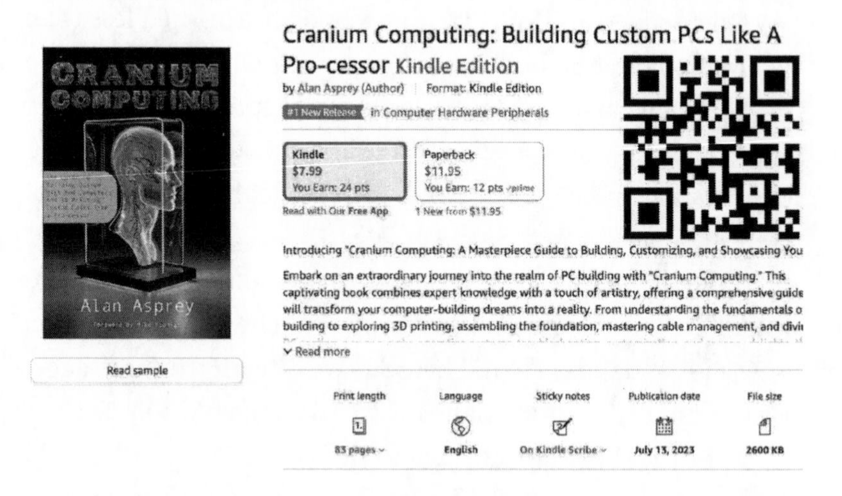

CRANIUM COMPUTING
Alan Asprey
Read sample
Cranium Computing: Building Custom PCs Like A Pro-cessor Kindle Edition
by Alan Asprey (Author) Format: Kindle Edition
#1 New Release in Computer Hardware Peripherals
Kindle
$7.99
You Earn: 24 pts
Read with Our Free App
Paperback
$11.95
You Earn: 12 pts
1 New from $11.95
Introducing "Cranium Computing: A Masterpiece Guide to Building, Customizing, and Showcasing You
Embark on an extraordinary journey into the realm of PC building with "Cranium Computing." This captivating book combines expert knowledge with a touch of artistry, offering a comprehensive guide will transform your computer-building dreams into a reality. From understanding the fundamentals o building to exploring 3D printing, assembling the foundation, mastering cable management, and divi
Read more
Print length
83 pages
Language
English
Sticky notes
On Kindle Scribe
Publication date
July 13, 2023
File size
2600 KB

And then I said, "What about a website?"

Alan said, "I don't know how to make a website."

I said, "Let's make one now." So we used another tool and built a website right there onstage in the middle of my presentation. The website was complete with all the sales copy, product images, mock-ups, and a cutting-edge web design–it looked better than some sites I've paid tens of thousands of dollars to create.

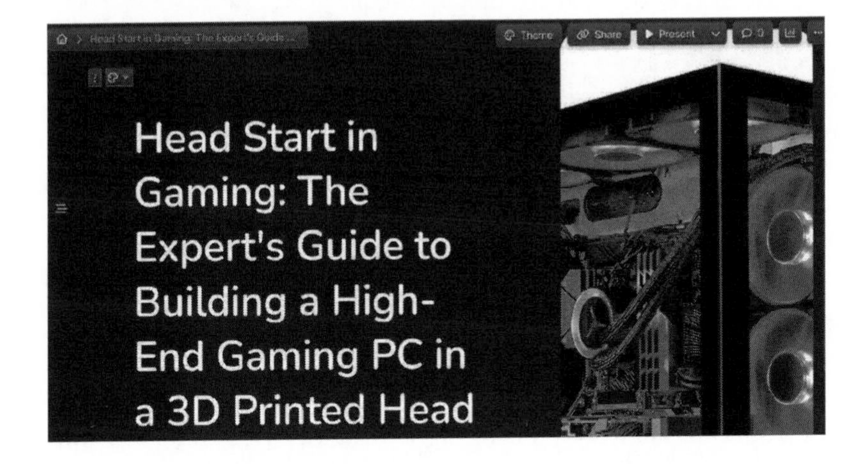

All of this is being seen in real-time by the audience.

Finally, after 15 minutes, I turned to the audience and said, "See what just happened there? In 15 minutes, we inspired a young man and created a business."

The Future of Education in an Ai World

Just imagine if kids aged 12, 13, or 14 learned how to create value, start their own businesses, make money, and even become wealthy before they're 18.

Instead of going to an institution that turns them into debt slaves for the rest of their lives, they could go to college to learn something. Instead of taking idiotic courses that infect their brains and make them anti-American, they could take classes that teach them the international language of peace and prosperity–entrepreneurship and value creation.

That's the vision of capitalism and the American dream I see.

You already know Ai is the next big thing.

I know you know because you've told me. I've delivered over 100 presentations to audiences of thousands of entrepreneurs just like you. During each presentation, I poll the audience using an Ai chat tool I'll show you later in the book. Thousands of entrepreneurs at events ranging from Tony Robbins Platinum Partners, Abundance 360 with Peter Diamandis, MIT, YPO, EO, CEO Alliance, Strategic Coach, Genius Network, and JJ Virgin's Mindshare Summit have told me what they want to know about Ai and how to implement it in their businesses.

Here are the top questions I get from founders:

1. How exactly do I get started with Ai?
2. What exactly should I use Ai for right now?
3. What Ai programs and apps should I use, and what can I reasonably expect Ai to do for me?
4. How PRECISELY do I bring Ai into my business so I don't have a mutiny or rebellion of fear and hostility?

Look, I get it. Ai creates a ton of confusion and fear in the business world because it's so new, radically different, and unbelievably powerful.

That's why I wrote this book. I want you to get past the confusion and BS and get straight to business...making money and creating value.

Here's the good news: I've designed this book specifically for you. You can read it in about 90 minutes, and by the end, you'll know where to start with Ai, guaranteed.

We've already identified over 30 areas of focus where Ai can instantly impact your business with super affordable or even free tools that can give you as much as a day per week back.

You can increase your team's effectiveness by two to five times, eliminate the need for expensive copywriters, and eliminate the need to add more people to your teams because they're more effective.

Ai gives you a way to get stuff done faster than it would take to describe it or delegate it.

More than that, you'll also see, maybe for the first time, how to leverage the three essential Ai mindsets–The Millionaire Ai Mindset™, The Billionaire Ai Mindset™, and The Trillionaire Ai Mindset™–to 10X or 20X the value of your business, and maybe even 100X the value.

You'll have a list of the most important apps, and if you scan the QR code on the next page, you'll get my personal, always-up-to-date list of the best, most powerful Ai apps that my team and I are using with our clients right now.

Thousands of Ai tools are released every day. My team and I are always on top of the best, most useful money-making tools as they are released. Go to https://www.MikeKoenigs.com/AiBookBonus or scan this QR code to get our specially curated list for entrepreneurs and business owners.

Having the list is cool, but you need a roadmap to know what apps and tools to start using and in what order.

Let's face it… employees and teams are justifiably afraid of this technology replacing them or taking away their jobs. Instead, they should embrace it because they can quickly become significantly more productive and more profitable, and reduce the time they spend on annoying, repetitive tasks, so they can add value in ways only humans can.

The Robots are NOT Here to Get You

I want to address this fear right up front. I don't buy into the fearmongering that you see in the media and from politicians who say that Ai is going to take over and we'll all be out of a job.

That's scarcity mindset, and I don't play that game. This book isn't for you if that's where your head is.

I'm not here to convince you that Ai is good–in the right hands, the hands of entrepreneurs who use it to create the next new products, services, and experiences that will transform our lives, Ai is the single biggest opportunity since the Internet.

And it's an order of magnitude bigger and better.

We're just at the very beginning, and I already know Ai technology will radically improve the quality of life, lifespan, health span, and wealth of humans on the planet. The only question is...will you play a role?

My Goals for You...

Here's my vision for you...the goals I want you to accomplish by the time you finish this book.

GOAL #1: Get Back Your Time

The first and best way to use Ai is to get back days and weeks of time. This isn't some productivity hack. I'm talking about exponentially cutting the time it takes to do everyday tasks in your business, like creating proposals, reports, marketing copy, social media, and more. You'll literally go from hours or days to minutes while increasing quality.

GOAL #2: Multiply Your (and Your Team's) Capabilities

In Chapter 4, I'll show you how to rethink your model for an Ai world. We'll "appify" your business so that all the "secret sauce" and voodoo magic you do for your clients and customers is baked into your own custom Ai. Now, your team can do all the stuff you thought only you could do. This shift alone will 10x the value of your business by removing owner dependence.

GOAL #3: See Your New IP Platform

Here is where it really gets interesting... Using The Trillion Dollar Idea Finder (a tool I'll show you how to use in Chapter 7), companies are quickly seeing how they can take their unique IP–the secret sauce that everyone lines up to pay them for, and package it inside an Ai platform, then sell it to their competitors.

You might be thinking, "Why would I want to sell my secret sauce to my competitors?"

It's the difference between being a prospector and selling "where to find the gold" maps. The guy selling the maps (and pickaxes and shovels) made a lot more (like 100x more) than most prospectors, and so will you when you make this new leap to package and leverage your IP that Ai enables.

The value of an IP or automation-driven company is 10x-20x REVENUE versus 2x-6x EBITDA. Ai-driven SaaS companies can be even more. You do the math.

When you get this, you'll unlock limitless opportunity for yourself and your business, and I'm so excited to share it with you.

Let's get this party started and push some wind in those sails!

P.S. Some people find my blunt and direct approach offensive. I may even use language that makes you blush. I polarize on purpose to create a reaction–you may love it, you may hate it. Either way, use that reaction to your advantage...ask yourself why you're reacting that way. I aim to challenge your thinking–you need that. Ai will challenge your thinking, and I'm going to push buttons intentionally to get you thinking bigger and differently. Those that do will thrive in this brave new world.

CH. 1

HOW AI WORKS (THE 2-MINUTE GUIDE FOR HIGH-QUICK START ENTREPRENEURS)

"You don't have to worry about Ai taking your job.
You do have to worry about someone using Ai taking your job."
— Peter Diamandis

Ai can help you invent, create, and launch a business or product in hours. Let that sink in for a moment. Think about the last time you launched a new product or service, website, marketing campaign, or even your business. How much time did it take?

I'm guessing weeks (at a minimum) and, in most cases, months or years.

When you really "get" what I'm going to share with you in this book, those limitations are gone. You are no longer limited by time, money, team, talent, transportation, distribution, or any other traditional barrier.

The new Ai future is one where you–your imagination–is the only limitation. How you approach this and the mindset you bring is going to be the key to your success. Scarcity mindsets or past traumas and fears are the things that will hold you back in the new Ai future.

10 Minutes to 10X Sales Productivity

Yesterday, I exported a file of over 870 records of complex information from a CRM database filled with unstructured text data that high-value prospects provided in a survey. Information about their business, biggest business challenges, opportunities, how they hope to use Ai to grow their business, and more. It was a LOT of data that normally would take days to process and turn into something useful.

I imported that file into ChatGPT with a simple prompt requesting that it give me the top 10 most valuable opportunities and challenges it discovered from the survey that could be turned into SaaS (Software As A Service) applications for the top 10 most valuable prospects in order of value, along with the contact information of each founder.

In less than a minute, I had my "hit list" of prospects and descriptions of what exactly they needed. I followed that up with a short prompt asking ChatGPT to write an engaging, upbeat, and persuasive email to each of those founders, mentioning that my team and I could help them achieve their goals.

That's about two days' worth of work done in less than 10 minutes. Soon, "agents" will learn this as a daily task and do it for you. Data analysis, research, sales, and marketing on autopilot.

Now, my team of "fractional Ai officers" can meet with each of these founders, brainstorm ideas with them, and build Ai solutions for them on the spot. We will find ways to clone the founder and their key employees. Plus, my team of Ai developers can rapidly develop commercial-quality apps in days or weeks instead of the months or years it used to take. In real-time we will save days or weeks and generate tens or even hundreds of thousands of dollars for each founder.

Remember when spreadsheets first hit offices worldwide? Overnight, analytical tasks that once demanded a room full of number-crunching nerds could be handled by a single person.

Productivity exploded.

Ai is going to change the game again, but this time in orders of magnitude. Here's how:

There are a couple of flavors of Ai, but the one that's going to have the biggest impact (and the one I'm going to show you in this book) is something called *generative Ai* - where Ai models create brand-new content like text, images, apps, and more rather than just organizing data.

These tools essentially give computers imagination and intuition, allowing them to assist humans in creative tasks.

How does this sorcery work? At the core are neural networks, massive webs of interconnected information structured like brains. By exposing these models to loads of data, they are trained by reading just about every bit of content that's been produced and is online, be it writings, conversations, images, or videos. Through reading this content, the computer finds the statistical patterns behind how the world works and how humans communicate ideas.

That's all big-brain computer scientist stuff. For us normal humans, we feed the system a text prompt, and it can generate whole paragraphs or stories in seconds...pretty cool!

Give it a description of an image you want, and it will draw, paint, and animate a brand new, 100% unique image for you. Supply keywords, and it designs mobile apps. Its knowledge spans everything from microscopic scientific processes to macro global affairs. And it never stops learning.

What Using Ai Looks Like In Practice

Picture an Ai that acts as a tireless personal assistant: scheduling meetings, answering routine client questions, processing paperwork, handling research, and even barking at telemarketers for you.

For marketers, imagine an Ai sketching out a storyboard for an animated marketing video the moment the idea pops into your mind, then making the video, complete with a voiceover in your voice.

For sales, what if you had an Ai that combs through all of your sales call transcripts to find exactly what works best to enroll clients, the best way to overcome a specific objection, or the most frequently asked questions in the sales process using the words of real prospects?

Name any business function, and there likely exists or soon will exist an Ai to enhance it. Unlike past automation revolutions, however, these tools empower human talents rather than replace them. Just like the invention of the calculator didn't erase the need for mathematicians, neither will Ai erase the need for uniquely human skills.

(No, Ai isn't coming for everyone's jobs…it's going to give us humans the ability to let the computer do the routine, monotonous stuff so that creative people will be exponentially more productive.)

An Ai can rapidly process millions of data points, but it takes human context to interpret what they actually mean for a business.

My friend Peter Diamandis is the first person I heard say, "Don't worry about Ai taking your job… You should worry about someone using Ai taking your job."

Adopting an Ai Mindset

Winning with Ai is a lot less about tech and a lot more about how you think. You're going to need to understand what Ai can do in general terms–it can do a lot, and it's getting more capable every day. You're going to need to take an open, "Hey, let's see if Ai can do this…" approach.

In Chapter 2, I'll share with you the three key mindsets you need around Ai: The Millionaire Ai Mindset™, The Billionaire

Ai Mindset™, and The Trillionaire Ai Mindset™. Together, you'll use them to get back a day a week in time for your entire team (maybe more), clone yourself and your best people, and 10X-100X the value of your business.

It's the shift in how you think that will make the difference.

How to Talk to Ai (aka Prompt Engineering)

I've asked thousands of entrepreneurs to share their questions and frustrations with Ai during the talks I give to high-level groups worldwide. One of the top frustrations is…

> *"How can I get past that blinking cursor that makes me look stupid? Every time I use ChatGPT or one of the new tools, I get terrible results, or the thing argues with me."*

You've got to learn the art of talking to the Ai, or what's called "Prompt Engineering." The good news is that it's simple. Once you learn a few basics, you'll have mind-blowingly productive "chats" where, for example, you can create a year's worth of marketing copy in less than 20 minutes without paying tens of thousands of dollars to a copywriter.

The Core Values that Make a Great Ai Prompt Engineer
• Curiosity
• Be a great generalist
• A willingness to experiment, iterate and stack prompts
• Knowledge of what's available
• An abundance mindset - nothing is impossible
• Time, money, people, education are not limiting factors

It's this big brain that has read most of the Internet, is constantly learning new stuff while you sleep, and, like a great assistant, is sitting on-call, waiting to help you. You just have to tell it what you want and understand that it might be a little quirky. You might need to clarify your instructions, redirect it (much like a real-life assistant sometimes), or give it more clarity.

Pretty cool. Let's get into it.

MINDSET: THE TRILLIONAIRE Ai MINDSET™

"The world's first trillionaires are going to come from somebody who masters Ai and all its derivatives and applies it in ways we never thought of."
— Mark Cuban

I was at Joe Polish's Genius Network (a mastermind group I've belonged to for over 12 years) event a few weeks ago, and a woman named Elaine walked up to me and said, "Mike, do you think you could help me with my book?"

I said, "Tell me exactly what you're looking for."

Elaine said, "Well, I plan on launching a book, but book launches are incredibly complicated. It will take me a long time, and I know I've got to write all sorts of copy. I've got to do lots and lots of interviews. I've got to do webinars and seminars. I need landing pages to capture leads and follow up with them."

I said, "I can imagine how terrible that is. How long do you think it will take, and how much will it cost to get all that stuff done?"

"At least two months, and will probably cost me $50,000."

I said, "Well, what if I could do it all with you right now, and we could get it done in less than 20 minutes?"

"I don't believe you, but it would be absolutely amazing if that were possible."

I sat her down and quickly composed a series of prompts for her. I used a new strategy I had just learned. In minutes, I trained ChatGPT to write:

- All of her book launch copy
- All of her follow-up sequences
- A list of questions she should be asked when she does podcasts promoting the book.

We also came up with a bunch of ideas for some great give-aways, as well as what she should sell on the back end.

I was able to copy and paste all of that information into a document and give it to her on the spot, along with an audio recording of our entire conversation so she could review it later.

I was able to do this so quickly because I had already done it before for myself. I had a template that I was able to copy and modify using her inputs. I told the Ai to replicate the template in the same format so it didn't have to be re-created again.

This is an idea we call blueprinting or creating playbooks. They are reusable templates and resources that we create once and use as a model. Then, we just train the Ai to remake them in the exact voice and style of a different business.

I said, "How much time and money do you think I just saved you?"

"That would have cost me $50,000 and taken me months of work."

That's right, artificial intelligence saved her $50,000 and completed months of work in twenty minutes. No waiting. No hassles. Faster than she could have communicated what she needed to a marketing consultant and copywriter or delegated to someone on a team she doesn't have. No contractors. No annoying mistakes. No missed deadlines.

But what's important here is that her business is still in the million-dollar-a-year range.

If you have a five million, a fifty million, or a five hundred million dollar business, that exact same strategy could be applied, except it would have a huge multiplier effect.

To leverage this incredible opportunity, you have to let go of the fear of running out, not having enough, and being limited by a lack of education, capabilities, people, resources, or time. Ai can erase all that...

The Ai Revolution

Before the Industrial Revolution, the majority of millionaires in the world were kings, their offspring, churches, and thieves who stole for a living. Then, entrepreneurs emerged for the first time during the Industrial Revolution, harnessing energy–steam, oil, and electricity–to get stuff done. Everything became better, faster, and cheaper, and the entrepreneurs who saw the possibilities became the world's first value-creation millionaires.

That lasted for about 140 years. Then, the Internet came along, and BOOM… We got billionaires. (Yes, we had billionaires before the Internet, but we got a lot more of those bad billionaires everyone loves to hate because of the Internet.)

Those old millionaires are great! Today's billionaires are great (the ones that aren't evil)! More billionaires, please!

When you create value by multiplying the effectiveness of lots of people, unimaginable things happen.

It's my opinion that Ai is going to create trillionaires soon–by the time you read this, it might have already happened. The Industrial Revolution took decades to create the millionaire tycoons–Carnegie, Rockefeller, JP Morgan, and others. The Internet Revolution took a decade to create Jobs, Zuck, Musk, and the Google guys.

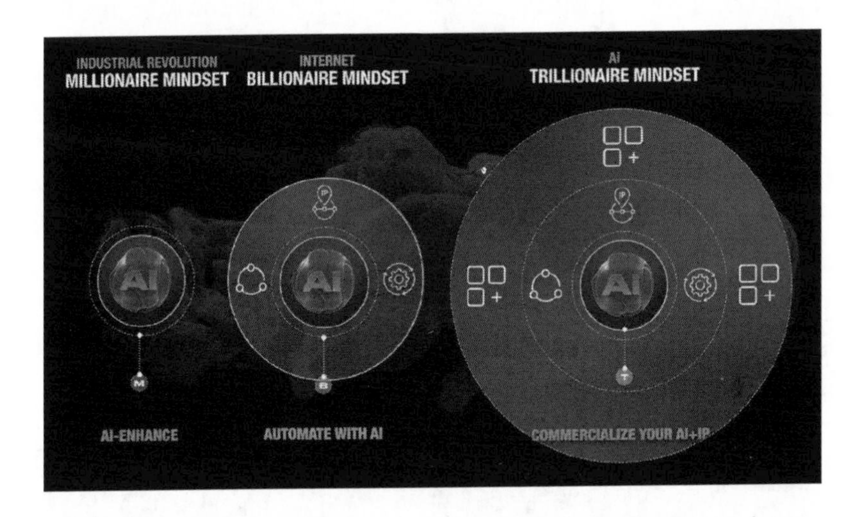

The Ai Revolution is going to be bigger and faster. Years, not decades.

Here's how it will happen and how you can apply this mindset to your own business starting today.

If you were to prep, scale, and sell your business, you'd get a multiple of Earnings Before Interest, Taxes, Depreciation, and Amortization...EBITDA.

Most businesses might get two and a half to five times EBITDA. But right now, if all you do is take some of the ideas and tools I'm giving you and apply the right kind of thinking (mindset), you could increase your productivity and your profitability by 20% to 200% in a brainless fashion.

It's stupidly easy…

I know it because I've been doing it with all my clients and everyone I'm working with. We're not using some super-techy Star Trek programming, just off-the-shelf tools that are mostly free or less than the cost of lunch on Tuesday.

The key to making piles of money with Ai is how you *think* about Ai using the three Ai Money Mindsets.

The Millionaire Ai Mindset™

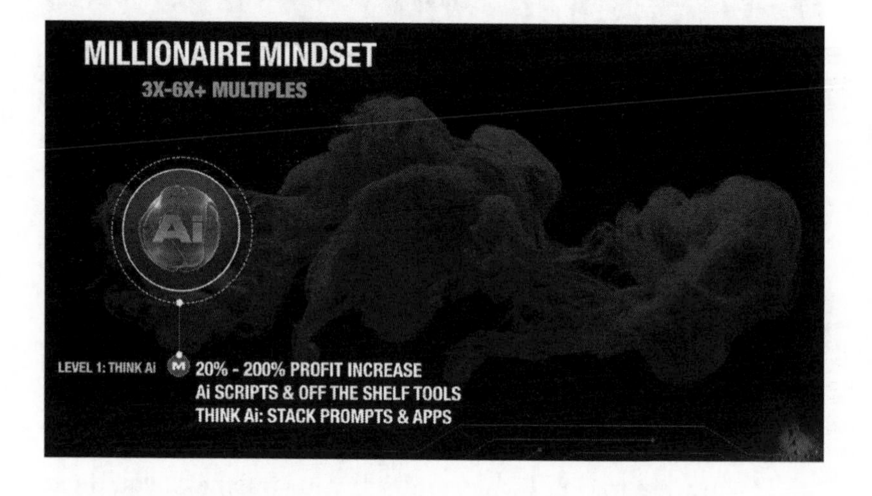

Just the very basic stuff you can do with Ai will add 7-figures to your business.

I'm talking about pure and radical productivity gains where you gain back one to two days per week starting right now.

What you want to do is spot the things you do over and over that you can teach someone on your team. If it involves writing anything, producing content, researching, or brainstorming, you're going to get more done in less time with fewer people with Ai on your team.

That's The Millionaire Ai Mindset.

That's how I was able to solve a $50,000 problem with Elaine in less than 20 minutes. And the next time I do it, I could probably do it in half the time, or one of my Ai consultants could do it so that I'm not even involved. Massive leverage.

Here's how I use The Millionaire Ai Mindset every day...

When I speak to an audience of top-level business owners, I survey them to find out what people want to do with Ai, even if they don't know what's possible or where to begin. One of the first practical mindsets in using Ai is just knowing what is realistic, what apps to use, and how to "stack" various systems to get the results you want.

Then, my team creates a step-by-step "recipe" to do that thing the audience said they wanted. We call them playbooks. They are copy-and-paste prompts (instructions) for an Ai like ChatGPT. Think of them as little Lego construction kits.

This is millionaire-level Ai thinking. Pretty simple but super powerful. Before there's an app, there's a little how-to book. One of the topics that comes up over and over in the surveys is "I want to write a book." We've created a playbook for that.

We've created dozens of these playbooks where you can copy and paste the instructions to the Ai. And it gets even better. OpenAi–the company that runs ChatGPT–has come out with something they call Custom GPTs (if you're wondering what a GPT is, it stands for Generative Pre-trained Transformer…yuck! You can tell the nerds named it).

Custom GPTs are like little apps anyone can create–no technical skill required. You take a playbook like we've created and paste the recipe into the custom GPT, give it a name, and now you have a little app you can share with your team or the public.

There's even a GPT store where you can get custom GPTs that other people have created to do all sorts of specific tasks. It's like the app store for the iPhone. There are already thousands of apps that solve virtually every problem imaginable for free or very cheap.

Here are some examples of the playbooks we've created, and all of these can easily be tweaked to your specific requirements and preferences and put into a custom GPT.

- Take a transcript of a conversation you have with a client and have the Ai write the follow-up email and a full proposal, following your own proposal format and language (because you taught it how you like to write proposals).

Let me stop there for a second... with just that one example of creating a follow-up and proposal, how much time do you think you would save? This is exactly how Jim Sheils, one of our real estate clients, slashed his proposal process from 40 minutes to 3 minutes.

His sales team can now talk to 35 percent more prospects per day. That's how you dramatically increase the productivity and profitability of every company. Everyone does more with less. That doesn't just increase revenue by 35 percent. That can go right to your bottom line without increasing expenses. In some businesses, that can double or even triple your NET profit.

Here are more examples of playbooks we've created (and my team is creating more all the time) that you can just copy and paste to save hours or days of work:

- **Billion Dollar Question** - Key questions to answer that dramatically increase your profitability, productivity, and team effectiveness and increase the value of your business, products, and services.

- **Publish, Profit Ai Book Writing** - Everything you need to write a book with the assistance of Ai.

- **Podcast Interview & Video Marketing Machine** - The fastest way to launch a podcast, create content, develop questions for guests, and rapidly produce all of your marketing materials and promotional materials for a show.

- **Create a Moonshot Business Plan** - If you were going to 10x or 100x your vision for your business, this is a construction kit to make your vision and dream for a more impactful future real.

- **Create a Product & Marketing Plan** - No matter what your business idea is, this plan will create an entire business and marketing plan in less than an hour, which would normally take weeks or even months to produce.

- **Profitable Course Creator** - Create entire courses and products in an afternoon that would typically cost tens of thousands of dollars and take a team weeks or even months to produce.

- **Signature Talk Toolkit** - One PowerPoint or Keynote presentation can generate $1 million in business in a single afternoon. This tool has been used to produce dozens of signature talks that can be used for stage, webinars, or even a TEDx talk.

- **Human Resources Recruitment Process** - Every business needs to hire more "whos" to get work done. Writing job descriptions and HR policies is a giant, expensive pain. This Playbook landed one of our clients a perfect-fit person for their COO role in one day using a want ad and hiring process created by Ai.

- **Build a Sales Organization in 10 Minutes** - The fastest way to grow a business is with great salespeople. Still, you need a well-tailored process and sales conversations to make those deals happen. These scripts and tools make it happen at record speed.

- **Sales Prospecting to Proposal Sent Guide** - What normally can take 20 minutes to 3 hours can be shortened into minutes with a set of scripts that emulate your best proposals combined with the hyper-personalization of ChatGPT.

- **Sales Proposal Follow-up Communication** - If you can't close your deals on the first call, you need a sequence of messages that keep your prospects engaged and interested and overcome their objections. This Playbook creates the messages for you, whether it's a year-long drip follow-up or a personalized 1-to-1 message..

- **Perfect Client System** - Without exception, organizations that aren't closing deals, don't really understand who their ideal customer is, and haven't figured out the proper messaging to reach them. In minutes, Ai will identify your perfect client's core pains, desires, and challenges so thatcan build a perfect avatar and close more deals.

- **Build a Brand Toolkit** - Communicate your brands, core values, purpose, and positioning to dramatically increase your perceived value.

- **High-Ticket Offer System** - Increase the price of your product by 3x-10x when you communicate more value. We've consistently helped our clients charge significantly more for the same product without changing the cost of delivery. This is a great way to tap into the hidden needs of your existing clients or prospects to communicate more value and better offers that deliver more.

- **SOPs in Minutes** - Businesses that have well-defined, standard operating procedures are significantly more efficient and have happier teams because they know what's expected of them. This Playbook turns ordinary conversations into standard operating procedures, and it allows you to model other businesses' systems and turn them into processes that you can use, saving you days or weeks compared to doing it on your own.

- **Social Media Marketing Machine** - You can easily model your competitors' best marketing, but change the message to mimic your voice or your brand's voice and generate weeks or months' worth of social media content in minutes.

- **Clone Yourself & Your Top Performers** - Imagine having a clone of yourself so that your team or customers could access your brain without you being there. Building a GPT or a robotic clone of yourself or your top performers to write content, advise, create proposals, or provide access to information so that you create massive leverage and new value in your business.

- **Write in Your Own Voice** - What if you could take your best content, proposals, books, brochures, website, information, or even social media posts to train a system that could then write in your voice on demand for all of your correspondence, emails, marketing materials, and more? How much time would that save?

How much leverage could you create for yourself? We built systems that have produced a year's worth of marketing content in less than an hour after creating a system with this playbook.

- **System KnowledgeBot Toolkit** - it's possible to clone all of the support content, FAQs, and customer service request emails and put them all in one place so they never have to be re-created ever again. This can reduce the number of support personnel you have on your team by 2/3 or even more. Our team has created knowledge bots that communicate in the voice of Brian Tracy, Ayn Rand, Dan Sullivan, and other professionals with extremely affordable tools that reduce employee count and work 24/7/365.

Full disclosure: I make it my life mission to survey every audience. I speak in front of and document every conversation I have with business owners. I analyze all of that information, constantly looking for opportunities to create more intellectual property and leverage that we can replicate and never recreate the wheel.

When I'm working with my clients, I do that in their business and try to find new ways to create value by leveraging their data and IP to build systems that can be worth more money than the actual business itself.

That's the point of the rest of this chapter.

Let's go bigger...

The Billionaire Ai Mindset™

The Billionaire Ai Mindset™ is taking your customized playbooks and "appifying" your business. This is how to 10x-20x the value of your business. Let me explain…

The #1 thing that makes it hard to sell a business is that the owner has his hands in everything. The business is *owner-dependent.* Who wants to buy a business like that? It's like buying a job, no thank you. That's why so many business owners have to work way longer than they want or sell for far less than they hoped.

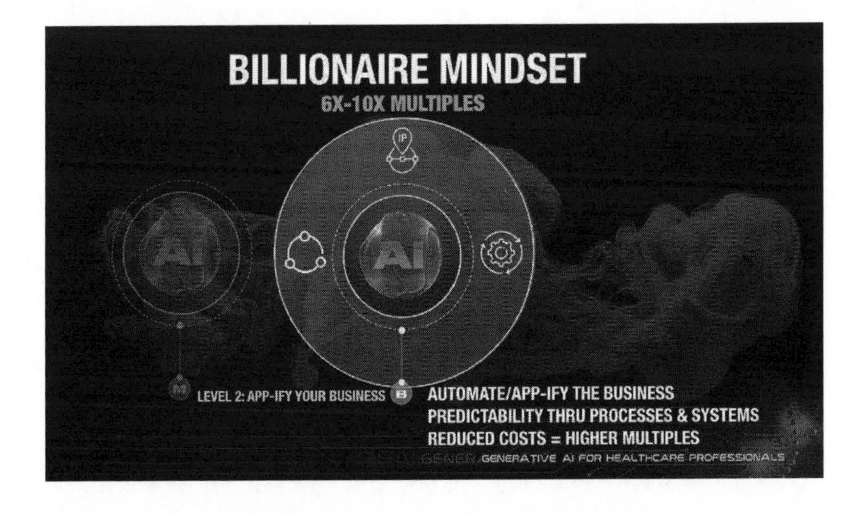

The Billionaire Ai Mindset™ changes that. You used to have to take all the magic tricks you do in your business that made it successful and slowly, painfully teach your people how to do the magic tricks. Then, just as one of them masters the show, she leaves. Go directly to jail, do not pass go, do not collect $200.

But now, you can teach the Ai your magic tricks, and it will do them faithfully over and over again. It never gets tired, never gets sick, never cops an attitude because it's the third Tuesday of the month, and the moon is rising over Taurus. It. Just. Works.

It's predictable and repeatable.

And for a potential business buyer, they look at that and think… It's all there, I don't have to worry about the key people leaving, I don't have to keep the old guy around for two years, it's all there, and it just works.

That's a business that buyers want. And, it's a business they'll pay a premium to get.

Now, I'm not saying you don't need good people. Ai is not going to replace them all, and that's not a world I want to live in anyway. But Ai will make you less dependent on key people. You'll be able to take even very complex processes and make them faster, yield more consistent quality, and scale them up with just a handful of people.

If you have apps that do the work of five or eight people, your company will be worth more when you sell it. You'll still sell for a multiple of EBITDA, but instead of a 2x-3x multiple, you'll jump to maybe 10x or 20x. It's a no-brainer.

Here's an example: we call it the DigitalCafe.Ai. In just two minutes, creates a personalized sales follow-up webpage and beautiful magazine-quality document speaking to a prospect's own goals, dreams, obstacles, and superpowers, a no-ring voicemail drop with a message in your voice, a custom video of you, speaking to the prospect, plus personalized follow-up emails and text messages–all generated by Ai for that specific prospect. Two minutes!

You answer six questions–just fill in the blanks–then it builds a beautiful, magazine-quality document that looks like this:

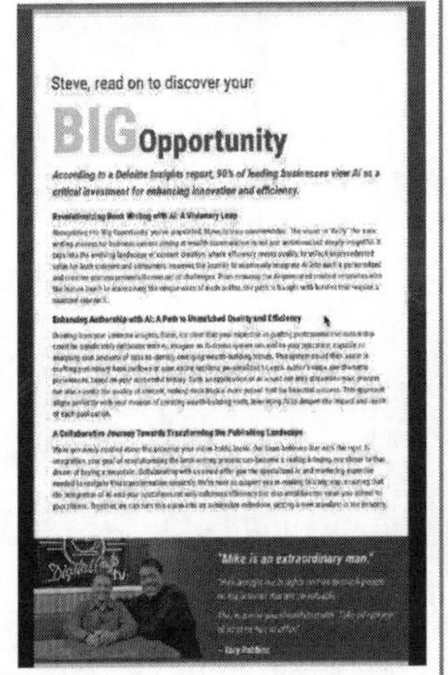

Build a Sales Organization in 10 Minutes

This is a Playbook and custom GPT that creates everything you need to design and manage your sales team so that they get better and better every month. It's a group of copy-and-paste prompts that ask you a series of questions. Give it your answers, and out pops everything you need to solve your biggest sales challenges. Here's an example of one of the prompts that gets the whole process in motion:

Current Sales Information

ChatGPT Prompt:
Act as a seasoned sales strategy consultant. Before moving on to tailored recommendations, I need you to ask me to provide you the following metrics about my current sales organization. Instruct me to enter all responses separated by commas and provide the list of questions in a numbered list format.

Number of Sales Reps: ____________
Revenue Goal for the Next 12 Months: ____________
Current Sales Cycle Length: ____________
Average Account Value (ACV): ____________
Current Close Rate: ____________
Monthly Budget for Operational Costs (excluding labor and commissions): ____________
On-Target Earnings for Sales Reps: ____________

Once you have this information, you will deliver comprehensive recommendations for optimizing my sales organization. These recommendations will address:

Talent acquisition and training
Sales process and methodology
Technology and tool stack
Incentive structures
Budget allocation

```
I expect your findings in a structured format, or-
ganized into separate sections for each focus area.
You will include actionable steps, potential road-
blocks, and KPIs to measure success. Your advice
will be precise and constructive.
```

ChatGPT will take this and the other prompts in the playbook and create the entire blueprint for your sales team:

- Your sales strategy
- How to hire people
- The KPIs for each individual
- What you should pay them
- The job ad
- The questions to ask candidates during the interview

This didn't take us long to create because all the knowledge is already inside Ai tools like ChatGPT and Claude.Ai.

These tools have been trained on about one-third of all of the content on the Internet, so basically one-third of all the knowledge of the human race.

To tap into all this knowledge, you just have to learn how to ask the questions and do the prompts. But even that's getting push-button easy because we're packaging these things.

Now, you're going to see in a moment how effective this is and where the big money is…

You have unique knowledge and experience that can be packaged and sold and not just be used by you. And that's The Trillionaire Ai Mindset™.

The Trillionaire Ai Mindset™

You're probably pretty happy by now–I showed you how to save at least two months of time per year (probably more) using the basics of Ai and the millionaire-level mindset. Then, I showed you how to eliminate owner and key-person dependence in your business, making it much easier and more fun to run and making it 10x-20x more valuable when you sell it.

But that's peanuts compared to what I'm about to show you–The Trillionaire Ai Mindset™.

Let's say you fix the problem and make your business twice as valuable. Do you think every one of your competitors would also love to have the same thing? Of course, they would!

We've been working with a client who has an auto dealership. He's sold $2.3 billion (with a "B") worth of cars. He's responsible for a half-million car transactions. That's a lot.

Now, there are 16,341 franchise auto dealers in the United States. Do you think they might want a plug-and-play system so that they start to operate more like our client's dealerships? Do you think that would make them a lot more money?

The first question we asked was, "Imagine if Ai and automation allowed you to have deeper, more meaningful relationships. How big would the impact be?"

If we actually made you more human and let a machine do machine things, how many more car buyers could you have a relationship with? That's my preference–the machine should do machine things to free up the humans to do more human things.

We analyzed the business and transcribed as much stuff as we could–sales conversations, marketing messages, SOPs, you name it. Then, we identified seven areas of focus that made his dealership better. Now, I will tell you that in your business, if there's something you do really, really well, that can be commercialized.

Interacting with a typical dealer stinks. The before-buying-a-car process stinks. The during-buying-a-car process stinks. The after-buying-a-car process stinks. If you're anything like me, you never want to wait on hold or talk to people. You'd like a machine to do all that for you and schedule it, remind you when something needs to be done on the car, so it's 100% handled, and you don't have to waste time. That'd be nice.

We decided that if he wanted to sell his whole process to other dealers as a service, with all the work to put it in place, he'd need a team of five to eight people–good people who he'd need to pay $80,000 a year or more. And most of them would fail, the turnover is very high, and replacing them is difficult. The typical HR problems we all have.

So, we designed an Ai app for all of that. To charge another dealer $10,000 per month for that tool would be a bargain. If he has 100 customers at $10,000 per month, that's $1 million per month–a million-dollar MRR.

The valuation of that kind of business with stable recurring revenue is 10x or 20x *revenue*, not EBITDA. A fast-growing software company is worth a hell of a lot more than a brick-and-mortar business. It's just the way it is. That's a company with a hundred-million-dollar valuation and just a hundred customers.

I don't know about you, but that's a damn good-looking business to me. Got it?

You already have this wisdom and knowledge inside of you–the secret sauce that makes you better than your competitors. It just doesn't mechanize now because it's dependent on humans. Program that knowledge, wisdom, and unique process into Ai, and that's where the trillion-dollar economy kicks in.

We're in the very early days. Much like the beginning of the smartphone era, things are going to change rapidly and in an even bigger way. To be successful in this new Ai age, we have to learn to think in Ai and dream in Ai. Now, the only thing that stands in our way is our ability to dream bigger.

MARKET: NO MARKET IS IMMUNE TO Ai

"Right now, people talk about being an Ai company. There was a time after the iPhone App Store launch when people talked about being a mobile company. But no software company says they're a mobile company now because it'd be unthinkable not to have a mobile app. And it'll be unthinkable not to have intelligence integrated into every product and service. It'll just be an expected, obvious thing."
— Sam Altman, co-founder and CEO, OpenAi

Ai can positively affect any market because it's relatively easy to make something better, less expensive, created and delivered faster, simplified, with fewer moving parts, and with less unwanted human engagement.

Anyone who thinks through that lens is going to win. To help you understand how to use this lens, I will give you a couple of real examples of how we've been using Ai through a market lens.

5x Sales With 20 Minutes of Work

Let me introduce you to Matt DiBara, fourth-generation masonry contractor and CEO of The Contractor Consultants. Matt has a unique challenge. He sells to building contractors.

I share the example because you're probably thinking, "How will contractors use and benefit from Ai?" Matt has an amazing system for hiring all the skilled and unskilled workers a contractor needs. He built it first in his own business, and now he teaches other contractors how to do it.

And, if you know any business owners in construction, you know they're always struggling to find, hire, train, and keep people. It's just terribly difficult right now.

Normally, having an HR person inside one of these companies who could run a system like Matt's would cost around $120,000 to $150,000 a year. Or, you could hire an outside head hunter, and they'll want a percentage of the salary of anyone they bring to you. Either way, it's usually way above what most contractors can afford.

Matt's got a great system, but his sales team struggled to enroll clients at a high enough rate. So I asked Matt, "Do you record your sales calls?" He did.

I decided I was going to use some of the new Ai tools I had been developing to analyze the sales conversations and see if I could create some new opportunities.

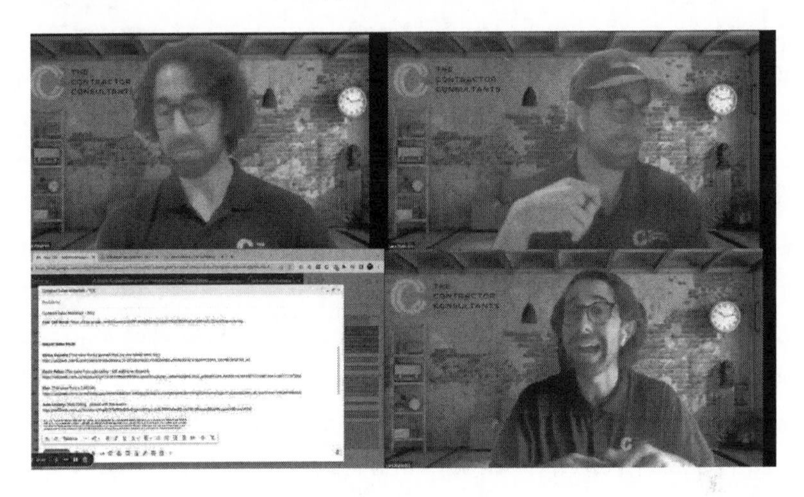

So here's what I did. I transcribed several sales calls, and I embedded a prompt I'd developed into a tool called Claude.Ai. I also gave it my book–*Punch The Elephant: How To Sell Anything To Anyone And Overcome Any Objection... Even If You're Bad At Sales*–which describes my super-effective sales process. (You can get the book by going to https://www.MikeKoenigs.com/PunchFree).

I asked the Ai to analyze the call logs and provide a detailed sales analysis, first comparing the calls to commonly known best practices for sales (which the Ai already knows because it's read the Internet). Then, I asked it to do another analysis based on my *Punch The Elephant* process.

Claude.Ai **Prompt: Review the following attached call logs and analyze them for sentiment analysis, and determine how to make each of these sales conversations more effective based upon phone and zoom-based sales best practices. Then analyze all of the sales conversations through the workflow and process described in the attached "Punch the Elephant" book manuscript. Then create a full report and analysis that can be shared with Matt DiBara from Mike Koenigs in his voice as the author of the punch the elephant book in the form of a step by step SOP that can be followed by a sales team. List key issues with their sales process, highlights, recommendations, ideas for improvement to improve and increase sales. Next in the form of a personal email, that is engaging, persuasive, visceral, and fun to read highlight all of the key things that should be done for each call.**

What happened next was nothing short of remarkable.

The recommendations were spot-on.

When Matt and his team employed my recommendations, their sales went from very low to very high, an improvement of about 80-percent in less than a week.

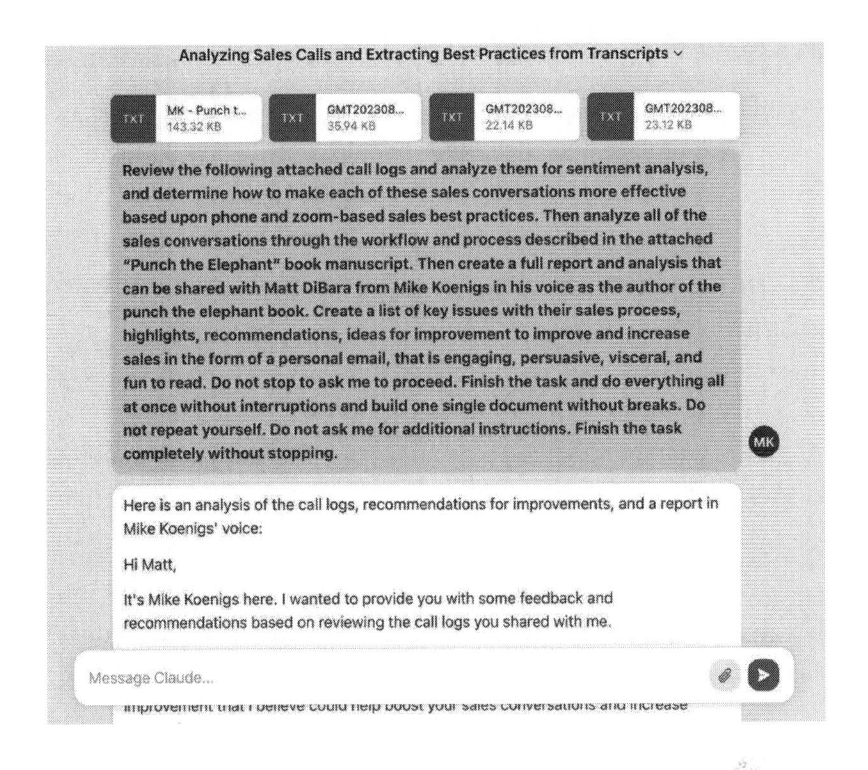

Now, if I had done this manually, it would have taken at least a day of my time to analyze and provide the reports. Even then, I still would have had to double-check my work or have someone else review it for me. Instead of 20 minutes, it would have easily taken two days of time, and it would have been very expensive time. And honestly, it's the kind of work that would've hurt my brain to do.

In fact, so expensive that Matt couldn't afford to pay me to do this for him.

This is important, so let me summarize: I took pre-existing call recordings, created a prompt that utilized business best practices for sales and information that I created in my own book, and asked for a report. It gave me fantastic results...in 20 minutes.

And now I have a repeatable system - in fact, I could turn this into a SaaS software solution and sell access to it to other sales teams. (And if you're wondering why I DON'T do this, it's because I'm currently focused on other more profitable business ideas).

I'm guessing that I have your attention if you're a business owner or founder. Imagine taking your own internal best practices for sales (or anything) and teaching the Ai how to analyze your team's performance, then writing a report to coach them to improve.

This is a very simple and basic example, but it's important because the businesses that embrace the Ai mindset will be better, faster, and more adaptable than their competitors.

Right now, using very little information and an Ai tool, you can easily identify, communicate, and learn about a market and then market to them very successfully with very little work.

Deep Analysis of Your Market

"Don't find customers for your product.
Find products for your customers."
— Seth Godin

With Ai you can learn more about a market in 5 or 10 minutes and either invent a product from scratch or improve something you already have. All based on real customer data you collect or data that ChatGPT already knows. With Ai you can know your customers better than every other business in your market.

In Chapter 1, I showed you how I took 870 records of complex customer survey data and, using Ai, pulled out all of the best, most valuable opportunities. Before ChatGPT, that same work would have been a giant pain in the ass. It would have taken at least a day, maybe more. You would have to take all of the free-form answers from the customers and build a way to categorize them, then filter by the value of both the idea and the prospect. It would have been a nightmare. And I wouldn't have been anywhere near as effective and finding the patterns. But I did it in 10 minutes, thanks to Ai.

Not only that, but the Ai wrote an email for me that I could send to each of the top 10 founders explaining how I could solve their #1 biggest, hairiest problem.

In 10 minutes!

If you're capturing survey data from your leads and customers, you now have a full-time data analyst working for you for $20 per month.

And, if you don't collect that data now, you can still learn more about your market than most competitors just by asking the Ai. ChatGPT has read most of the Internet. It is constantly being updated with the latest new content, so it knows what your ideal prospects are thinking and feeling when it comes to what you sell.

You just have to know how to ask it. Now, let's take Matt's market, contractors. Let's ask ChatGPT to teach us about the market by giving it this prompt.

ChatGPT Prompt: I'm a consultant to general contractors, and you're my marketing strategist. I want to understand the 10 biggest challenges that owners or founders of construction companies are worried about when it comes to their business. Then, I want you to give me a list of the 10 biggest changes coming to the construction industry that will create new opportunities in the next decade.

ChatGPT Response:

The 10 Biggest Challenges for Owners/Founders of Construction Companies

1. **Labor Shortages and Skill Gaps:** The construction industry often faces difficulties in finding skilled labor, which can delay projects and increase costs.
2. **Rising Material Costs:** Fluctuations in the cost of materials can impact budgeting and profitability.
3. **Regulatory Compliance and Safety Standards:** Navigating the complex landscape of local, state, and federal regulations poses a significant challenge.
4. **Project Management and Efficiency:** Ensuring projects are completed on time and within budget requires sophisticated management tools and practices.

5. **Technology Adoption:** Integrating new technologies into traditional construction processes can be difficult but is necessary to stay competitive.
6. **Sustainability and Green Building Practices:** Adapting to the growing demand for sustainable construction methods requires new skills and knowledge.
7. **Supply Chain Disruptions:** Recent global events have highlighted the vulnerability of supply chains, impacting project timelines.
8. **Competition and Market Saturation:** Standing out in a crowded market is increasingly challenging for construction companies.
9. **Client Acquisition and Retention:** Building and maintaining a solid client base is crucial for long-term success.
10. **Financial Management and Access to Capital:** Managing cash flow, financing projects, and accessing capital can be complex and is crucial for growth.

The 10 Biggest Changes Coming to the Construction Industry

1. **Digital Transformation:** The adoption of technologies like Ai, IoT, and big data for smarter project management.

2. **Sustainable Construction:** A shift towards more eco-friendly materials and energy-efficient building practices.
3. **Prefabrication and Modular Construction:** These methods will increase efficiency and reduce waste, transforming how buildings are constructed.
4. **3D Printing:** Offering new possibilities in custom designs and on-demand material production.
5. **Augmented Reality (AR) and Virtual Reality (VR):** For enhanced planning, training, and visualization of projects.
6. **Robotics and Automation:** Automating repetitive tasks to improve efficiency and address labor shortages.
7. **Smart Contracts and Blockchain:** For more transparent and efficient contract management.
8. **Wearable Technology:** Improving worker safety and productivity through smart wearables.
9. **Green Technology and Renewable Energy:** Integration in construction projects to meet regulatory and societal demands for sustainability.
10. **Data Analytics and Predictive Modeling:** For better decision-making and risk management in construction projects.

That was with one simple prompt and about 45 seconds of ChatGPT thinking and writing. As I'll show you in Chapters 5 and 6, you can take these challenges and opportunities and create a year's worth of marketing in minutes that speaks precisely to your ideal client's biggest threats and opportunities.

I can even take this a step further and create prompts that help me design high-value products and services for this market based on the highest-value and highest-priority problems they have.

Then, I can give the tool instructions to start designing and actually creating those products, including writing code. Taking another step further, as you'll see in the next chapter about Message, I can create all of the marketing campaigns to launch and promote that product.

My team and I can build an entire product and service, prototype it, and launch it in a matter of days. That's what "The Superpower Accelerator" business does. We imagine, create, build, and deploy entire businesses end-to-end in a week.

In some cases, we prototype and develop software that is fully functional in that same week. We are frequently going from idea to over $1 million in revenue in less than 100 days.

We've had several clients leave my beach condo where we develop these businesses, fly to a meeting or event the following day, and close over a million dollars in sales on a brand-new business or product we created. In two cases, the clients sold over $1 million in sales on AN IDEA just 24 hours after we created it.

The key is knowing how to leverage the Ai mindset and adapting it to your market. The next two chapters explain how this is done.

Then, we'll talk more about how you can do it and apply all of these mindsets and tools in your business.

CH. 4

MODEL: SIMPLER AND FEWER DOESN'T MEAN LESS

"Most companies are built to execute today's business model, not discover tomorrow's."
— Scott D. Anthony, Managing Director at Innosight

In the fall of 2009, I stood in a parking lot in La Jolla, California, to meet Sam. Sam was referred to me by a friend.

She rolled up in a Tesla Roadster. Tesla didn't have showrooms. Just salespeople who drove model cars to parking lots to meet people like me. Sam sold Teslas.

I put my son Zak, who was six then, in the passenger seat. I sat behind the wheel, and Sam gave me the sales pitch for the car…"Floor it!"

We pulled out of the parking lot, and I did what I was told. Holy SHIT! Zero to sixty in 3.7 seconds. What a turn-on… That car was f@@king fast! And quiet. I looked at my six-year-old. Both of us were giggling with ear-to-ear grins. I had one thought on my mind: "This thing is so much fun it should be illegal." It was just like driving a slot car - and it sounded like one, too.

We drove to my favorite La Jolla road: Ardath Road—the best curve in San Diego for 100+ mph sports cars. You feel like you're at the beginning of a loop on a roller coaster.

This doesn't make me a good dad, but I drove over 100 miles an hour in that little Tesla Roadster and was awestruck. Mind blown. This thing was sex on wheels. If you've ever shot a machine gun or jumped out of a plane, both of those come close to what I was experiencing.

So, 15 minutes later, I returned to that parking lot and ordered a $125,000 car on the spot.

No dealers, no bullshit. Take it or leave it.

I fell in love with Tesla because I loved that sales pitch, and I'm a sales guy who's a sucker for a good pitch.

I loved the experience of not haggling with a car dealer or going around and around with a commissioned salesperson who wasn't operating in my best interests. F**k that. Come to me and sell me a car with two words. Then, do all the paperwork for me. That's it.

The price was the price. It was worth every penny. I drove that car HARD every time I got into it and made a point of giving everyone "The Tesla Grin" when they took the passenger seat.

Tesla disrupted the car-buying model. I was such a fan that I produced a documentary called "Life With Tesla" (you can still watch it at www.LifeWithTesla.com) and managed to deduct the car and my entire solar panel installation on my house as a "production expense." Free car. Free solar. Free Tesla Grin.

That's why I love capitalism. It's all about getting shit done. Convenience. Shortcuts. Workarounds. Creating and getting good deals. Not just thinking outside the box. Smashing the box. I love a big bonfire - burning old stupid stuff like bureaucracy, unions, and politics that sucks the life out of fun and the fun out of life

Capitalism is all about applying everything you have–knowledge, experience, expertise, capabilities, collaboration, resources, and efficiency–to find a better way and then commercialize it.

Competition creates better humans, and the market is beautifully unforgiving. It doesn't speak crybaby. It got an "F" in sensitivity training.

The market votes for whatever is in its best interest and according to its values, whether it's price, quality, personalization, speed, political or religious belief, being green, or some messaging story that inspires that buyer. Buyers don't always make great decisions, but they are making decisions, and as business owners, it's our job to create a business model that works with the product, service, or experience to deliver what they want (even if they don't know they want it yet).

Tesla is successful because it took an old process that nobody likes and figured out a better way. They pulled out all the B.S. and made it simple. Look at Tesla's valuation. As I write this, they are valued at more than 2x the closest competitor, Toyota, and have reached a market cap of over $1 Trillion. Elon says and does some stupid stuff, but I wouldn't bet against him.

Same with Uber. They applied The Billionaire Ai Mindset,™ and now they're valued exponentially more than any taxi company on the planet. They're easier to use for customers and more convenient, and they've completely disrupted an entire industry.

It's the same reason I love Ai. Ai makes it easier than ever to create a new model, even in old crusty industries like the automotive industry and the taxi business. I'm glad I never again have to get a ride in a nasty car that smells like BO with a guy with a bad attitude.

Are you getting it?

Let me show you another example–my own. This is how I'm applying a new model to an old industry–the marketing/branding/advertising business.

For the last 100 years, if you wanted a world-class brand and all the marketing collateral to go with it, you hired a marketing/branding agency. Some companies spend millions and waste years working with an agency to get this done. If you speak with most business owners, they'll still say something like this:

"I'll meet with a marketing agency or my internal marketing and branding team. They take notes. They go away. A few days or a few weeks, they come back, and it's still wrong."

We flipped that model on its head. We do everything in real time. There's no waiting. No homework.

My two favorite words are DONE and NOW.

When I work with business owners and founders to create their Next Act, they come and stay at my condo on the beach in La Jolla, California, with a co-founder or spouse. It's a beautiful, magical environment to work on your business. The ocean is inspiring.

When you arrive, we spend three days together and walk away with a whole new product, a whole new business, a brand, and all your marketing and content.

Not weeks, months, or years...three days.

Now, you might be wondering, why am I telling you all this, and what the hell does it have to do with Ai?

Real-world use cases.

The point of the example is that my team and I can do the work that normally takes a team of six people three to six months in just three days. It just isn't or wasn't possible without Ai.

Two weeks ago, we created two years' worth of marketing campaigns in about half a day by building a series of "Ai Playbooks" - step-by-step, paint-by-numbers instruction manuals that humans can use to talk to Ai. I will walk you step-by-step through how we did it in Chapter 5.

In other words, we digested the founder's voice by grabbing all kinds of content that we had created with them and for them right there in those three days at the condo. We fed it into an Ai and taught it how to speak in the founder's voice.

Then, we gave it some basic instructions and ways of writing and reading.

Next, with a series of prompts, which we documented step by step, we produced huge volumes of content.

But again, it took about half a day to create the content. That beats the hell out of months of work. And the best thing is, it's repeatable.

That company now doesn't need us to write their next 52-week email marketing campaign or all their follow-up content whenever they do an event. They can take a B or a C-level employee with basic marketing skills, feed the prompts we gave them into one of the popular Ai platforms, and get results.

Last week, we did the same thing again, except this time, we built a custom GPT that we trained, and it produced a 52-week email marketing campaign in about an hour. That B or C-level employee doesn't need to copy/paste prompts now–they just say, "Write a 52-week email campaign for product X," and the tool spits it out in minutes.

That one bot replaced the need for one to two full-time copywriters and did work that would normally take at least three weeks. The estimated value of that work is $30,000 to $75,000.

And I'm going to repeat what's important here.

We did that in about an hour. A month from now, it'll probably take 20 minutes. Maybe less.

The New Rapid Prototyping Advantage

Now, we've added rapid application prototyping to our three-day process.

While we're working on a brand, we'll find ways to rapidly prototype software that can automate business processes, like copywriting, and look for ways to leverage and commercialize that technology for that industry.

That's The Trillionaire Ai Mindset™ at work, by the way.

It used to take my previous companies months to design, prototype, beta test, and release software. That's the work of two lead developers and four junior and support engineers, 6 to 8 weeks (minimum), and hundreds of thousands of dollars. Now, it can be done in 48 to 72 hours, sometimes less, by one developer.

My wife, Vivian, says, "You finally have tools that can keep up with your imagination."

Again, this is the Model.

Ask yourself this question, "How can Ai completely change, improve, and automate all of the most challenging parts of my business, giving me ways to increase my NET profit 2x-5x or more without adding more people, complexity, or costs?"

What Ai Means for Your Team

Thanks to the media and the dirty politicians (ok, they're not all dirty!), your team is probably running scared, thinking the robots are coming for their jobs. And if you read what I just wrote, where we cut team size by 70-90 percent, you might think the doom and gloom media is right.

It's good news and bad news for your team. For your A-players, you can give them a dream come true experience–you're going to focus on the stuff you love, the stuff that you're great at, and we're going to give the Ai all the boring, repetitive shit. They're going to work less and make more money because they're making you more money.

For your B-players and C-players, you're going to give them a way to be three times more productive and valuable. They'll be able to create things that before had to be done by A-players or by you. You're effectively going to make them A-players when they pair with Ai.

That's what Ai is all about.

How to Apply The Trillionaire Ai Mindset™ to Your Model

Here's how to put this to work in your business.

Step 1 - Ai-ify Your Business: You want to create the equivalent of a playbook, a step-by-step instruction manual with the scripts, prompts, and tools that increase your value. You need to find a way to decrease labor that normally takes days, weeks, or even months of time to less than a day, then half a day, then two hours, and then an hour.

Step 2 - Appify Your Business: Now appify those processes so you have "black box" tools with your unique knowledge, wisdom, and processes embedded in them so that your team can use them. You want it to be easy to use, understand, and produce the desired outcome. You'll cut your dependence on key people.

Step 3 - Commercialize Your IP: Now, think about how you can turn that IP into a platform or a commercial product. A SaaS version of your business is worth 10x-20x multiples of revenue, not EBITDA. When valued correctly, the DATA in your business is worth 4x more than the business itself.

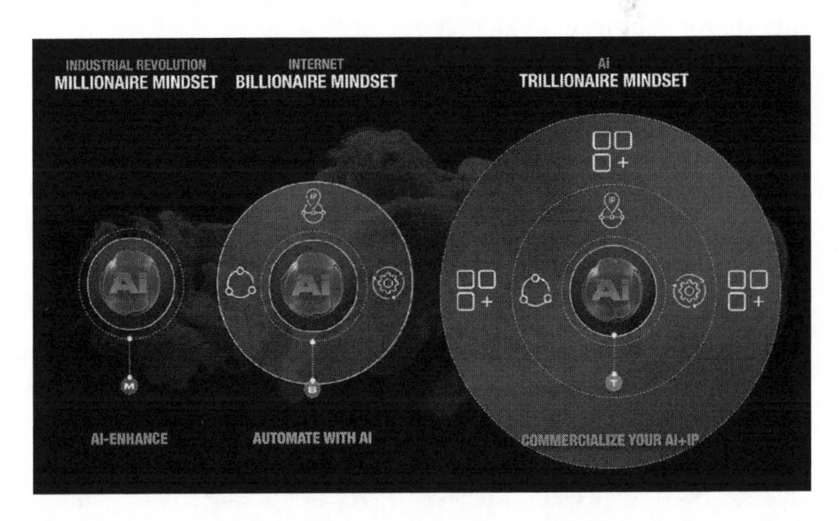

This is also known as eating your own young, which basically means you can say, "I'm going to Ai-ify my business. Next I'm going to appify my business, and then I'm going to go out and sell that IP as a product to my competition." The value of that could easily be 10 to 20 times the value of your revenue as long as there's a market for it.

I believe that is the key to creating massive multiples in the future.

Based on this model, we are currently building software tools in real estate, longevity, healthcare, telecommunications, wealth management, fitness, and nutrition. In every case, the founders of these companies realize that we can use Ai to increase their revenue dramatically. Then, augment or replace key people. Then, commercialize that system or process and sell it to an audience of hundreds or thousands of customers for $1,000, $5,000, $10,000 per month or more to create recurring income. Then, exit by selling that business to private equity or get acquired by a strategic buyer.

Let's do the math:

Just 100 customers at $10,000 per month = $1 million MRR (monthly recurring revenue)

That's $12mm ARR (annual recurring revenue)

And the right buyer will pay 10x-20x REVENUES for that business.

That's $120mm-$240mm for a business with 100 customers.

That gets really interesting when you have 1,000 customers, right? Mind-blowing.

This is a critical moment for you because founders who don't adopt this mindset will likely find it impossible to catch up with their competitors who started using Ai first. It's one of the reasons why it's going to become nearly impossible for other chipmakers to catch up to Nvidia. The more you use Ai, the faster you evolve and create an impenetrable moat around yourself.

Here's another example:

You know how businesses are notoriously bad at follow-up? We built an Ai-app that immediately researches prospects when they inquire or interact with your business and follows up with them in minutes with totally customized, completely personalized email, audio, PDF brochures, and even videos, with the intention of automatically setting an appointment.

My vision is to commercialize that product and license it to clients and customers with the goal of producing a $10 million or even $100 million exit for ourselves based on this technology.

It's my opinion that this could be done in virtually any business category.

To be clear, what we mean when we talk about Ai-ifying a model is first to use Ai to dramatically increase productivity and reduce dependency on difficult-to-find-or-replace humans. Then, we automate those productivity gains by appifying the business so that people can be focused on doing people-related, connection, and relationship-oriented things that machines can't do.

Finally, commercialize what you've created for yourself every step of the way, creating substantially more value.

CH. 5

MESSAGE: CREATE A YEAR'S WORTH OF MARKETING IN 2 HOURS

"The most powerful person in the world is the storyteller. The storyteller sets the vision, values, and agenda of an entire generation that is to come."
— Steve Jobs, Co-Founder, Apple

What would it be worth to you to write a book with your son, daughter, sibling, parent, or partner…or just get one done for yourself?

This is my 19th book, but I will tell you about my 18th.

I co-authored Book 18 with my 20-year-old son Zak, using an early version of ChatGPT in less than two weeks. If I had been able to keep him focused and disciplined, it could've been done in two days. But his ADHD is worse than mine, and following directions and getting up on time isn't part of that frontal lobe as of yet.

However, no matter what your circumstances, I'm going to give you a formula that could help you write a book in a couple of days or weeks with little or no experience.

For more than 20 years, I wanted to write a book about interviewers and interviewing. I grew up watching Johnny Carson, David Letterman, the Dick Cavett Show, Merv Griffin, and Oprah. They were masters.

I was inspired to become a great interviewer, too. In the tiny town of Eagle Lake, Minnesota, where I grew up, I dreamed of sitting on stage with comedians, Hollywood actors, musicians, and legends. I'd sit in the basement with my dad's reel-to-reel tape recorder, record my own mock TV shows, and pretend I was Johnny Carson. When my dad came home with what was a brand-new cassette recorder, I immediately took it over and started recording my own audio show that I called "Wack-o" - my version of the Muppet Show. I made up all sorts of strange cartoon voices and did all of the characters myself.

Many years later, after building a production studio, I started doing my own podcast interviews and online TV shows. I needed to learn the art of interviewing, so I researched every interviewer I could get my hands on and read as many transcripts as I could. I spent years digging around in libraries, studying and watching shows, and taking hundreds of pages of notes.

At one point, I committed myself to writing a book of the top 25 best interviewers from TV, radio, and magazines, finding the top 25 podcast and YouTube interviewers, and creating a list of their top 25 questions.

I quickly realized that would take months of research. I contacted a talented researcher I knew who quoted me $60,000 just to compile all this information. That didn't include writing the book. More than 10 years went by.

When ChatGPT was released in November 2022, I tried out an idea that took 10 minutes and wrote a chapter of that book. While doing that test, my 20-year-old son Zak called me from college and asked if I had something he could do to make some money. He wanted to see a concert with his friends that weekend and was out of cash.

I told him to jump onto Zoom with me, and as long as he agreed to follow directions, do exactly what I told him to do, and stick to a deadline, I'd pay him $20 per hour to co-author a book with me. He accepted the challenge, and this is what I gave him:

ChatGPT Prompt:

Create a list of the top 25 best interviewers from TV, radio, and magazines

Create a list of the top 25 podcast and YouTube interviewers

- **Next, write a chapter by answering these 4 questions:**
- **What inspired them to become an interviewer?**
- **How did they learn how to be a great interviewer?**
- **Who were their mentors?**
- **What is considered their best 25 interview questions?**

Write an intro for ____________ to a chapter of a book about great interviewers.

```
Midjourney Prompt:
Howard Stern as a line drawing in the style of
Atlantic magazine
```

(Midjourney is an Ai tool that creates graphics based on a text description you type in, like the one above.)

Together, we wrote this chapter of the book together in about an hour, including making this image:

Howard Stern

Howard Stern is a name synonymous with the art of interviewing. He is a radio and television personality, producer, author, and actor who has spent over four decades entertaining audiences with his unique interviewing style. Stern's interviews are famous for their candidness and ability to bring out the most unexpected responses from his guests. He is often credited with revolutionizing the talk radio format and is regarded as one of the most influential personalities in the history of broadcasting.

What inspired Stern to become an interviewer?

Howard Stern has always been drawn to the world of broadcasting. As a child, he was fascinated by the voices he heard on the radio and would often mimic them. In his early years, he was exposed to the work of radio legends like Steve Allen, Arthur Godfrey, and Jack Benny. Their ability to captivate audiences with their wit and humor inspired Stern to pursue a career in broadcasting.

How did Howard Stern learn to be a great interviewer?

Stern's journey to becoming a great interviewer was not a linear one. He started his career as a disc jockey in college and eventually landed a job at a local radio station. Over time, he developed his unique style of humor and storytelling, which he then brought to his interviews. Stern has often credited his time as a stand-up comedian for teaching him the art of timing and delivery, skills that have become a hallmark of his interviews.

Who were Stern's mentors?

Howard Stern has cited several personalities as his mentors throughout his career. One of the most notable is the late Don Imus, who mentored Stern during his time at WNBC in New York City. Imus taught Stern the importance of staying true to his own voice and encouraged him to take risks and push boundaries. Other personalities who influenced Stern's career include Larry King and Johnny Carson.

What are considered Howard's best 25 interview questions?

1. What was the defining moment of your childhood?
2. How did you get your start in your career?
3. What's the most embarrassing thing that's ever happened to you?
4. Can you describe your relationship with your parents?
5. What's the most significant risk you've ever taken?
6. What's the biggest mistake you've ever made?
7. Can you describe a time when you were faced with a difficult decision?
8. What motivates you to keep going when things get tough?
9. What's the biggest misconception people have about you?
10. What's the most significant lesson you've learned in your life?
11. Can you describe a time when you felt completely out of your depth?
12. What's the most challenging thing you've ever had to overcome?
13. What's the most significant sacrifice you've ever made?
14. Can you describe a time when you were genuinely happy?
15. What's the biggest regret you have in your life?

16. What's the most important thing you've learned about yourself?
17. What's the biggest challenge you're currently facing?
18. Can you describe a time when you failed and bounced back?
19. What's the most significant change you've undergone in your life?
20. What's the most important relationship in your life?
21. What's the most valuable lesson you've learned from someone else?
22. Can you describe a time when you had to make a difficult compromise?
23. What's the biggest misconception you had about yourself?
24. What's the most significant thing you've learned about human nature?
25. Can you describe a time when you felt completely in control of your life?

And then, every time I spoke on stage, I told the story about how I inspired my 20-year-old son to co-author a book with me, how it was done, published, and a #1 bestseller inside of two weeks, and how I also agreed to give him all of the royalties for that book.

What had more impact was how dozens of parents with kids in their late teens and early 20s would walk up to me with tears in their eyes, saying, "I wish I could inspire my kid to do something like that. Is there any way you can coach him/her or create an entrepreneurial program for young people?"

A few months later, Zak even started his own business, creating audiobooks with the help of Ai. He was quickly earning upwards of $10,000 per month.

To me, this is one of the greatest success stories of my life, both as a parent and creator. Now, when I tell this story, I get asked by parents and young people to help them start their own Ai businesses.

And yes, it's my intention to create a program for young people. I need to get a few things off my plate this coming year first...

Make Ai Write Like You

Imagine you had your very own Ai-driven app–a custom GPT–that knew all of your content, understood exactly how you liked to phrase certain things, and learned to write in your voice, so even you couldn't tell the difference.

We did that for Dr. Laura, one of our clients. We gave the Ai voice the instructions from our "Write in Your Own Voice" Ai Playbook. We loaded in the business description, the avatar (who we are writing to), and what's important to them. Then, we gave the Ai knowledge about the business and its messaging (this is known as training. In this case, we loaded in testimonials, a book, and a short TED talk-style presentation the client had given.

Now, you can simply click a button, and the custom GPT will give you relevant, contextually accurate, and valuable content, marketing emails, website copy, and social media posts that are all in the owner's voice. He doesn't have to write them ever again! He can hand that custom GPT to an intern, and they can do all of his marketing copy for him in minutes.

Let me repeat that... he can hand that custom GPT with his voice and his brain embedded in it, and the intern can create virtually any kind of marketing copy at the same level of quality, or at least very, very close to it, as the owner.

And, in case you're thinking, "That must have been hard to build," we built it in about an hour with no techy dudes involved. Literally, copy-paste with a command.

As of the time of this writing, here's how easy it is to build a custom GPT that can write in your voice and save you tens (or even hundreds of thousands of dollars) per year in copywriting and hours, days, or weeks of frustration.

Go to https://chat.openAi.com/ and click on "Explore GPTs," then "+Create":

Then you'll fill in this information - the only box that really matters is "Instructions":

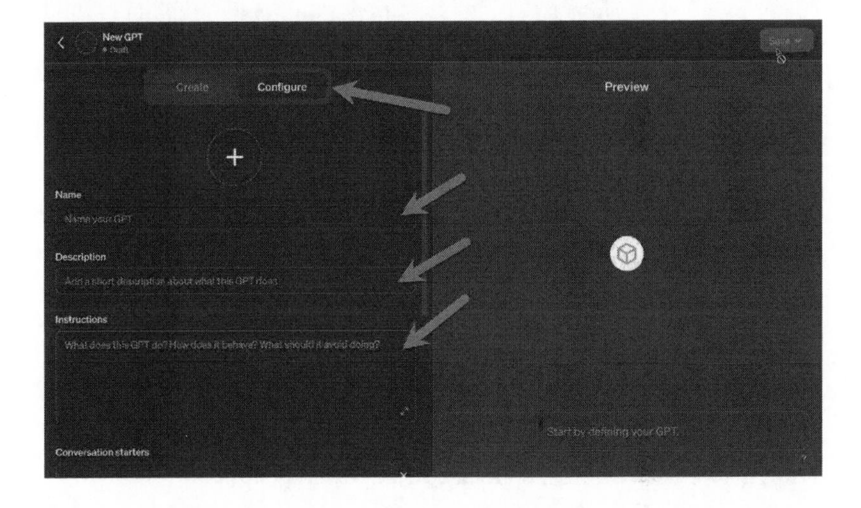

This is my "no homework" approach to using Ai. Your initial reaction might be, "That sounds like it'll be horribly difficult to train an Ai to speak in my voice," but it turns out that you can show the Ai something that's already working and then tell it to copy that model, but instead insert your information in its place,

Let me give you a good example of how easy it is to create a copywriting bot that writes in your voice.

We begin by copying the instructions from one of our previous clients and then uploading 2 to 20 documents written in our voice, such as articles, books, emails, newsletters, or even interviews and conversations.

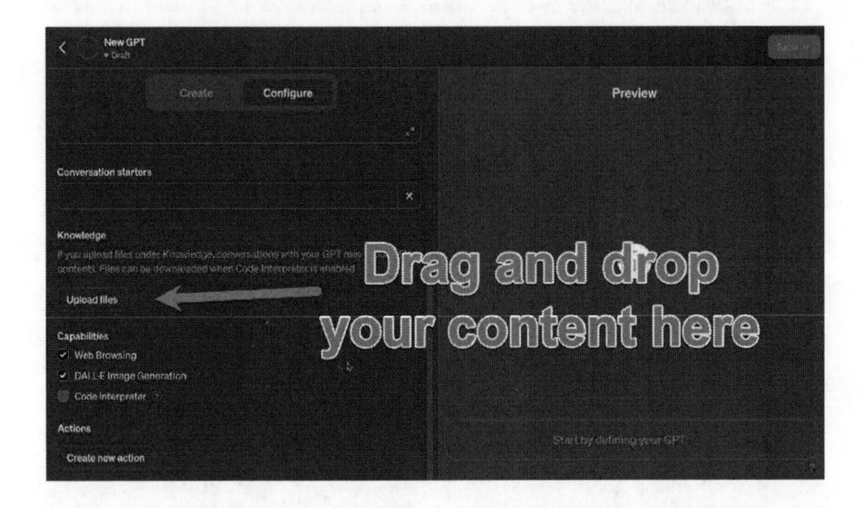

Your content can be taken from transcription programs, such as Otter.Ai, Read.Ai, or any of the dozens of other tools you might use for transcribing or recording content.

You simply copy this template along with an instruction that says to read all of the attached documents and then rewrite the instructions but modify them for you. In about a minute, that process is done, and you have a copyright system that is approximately 85% accurate and gets better in a couple of hours with a little extra tuning.

This is my "instruction set":

"Write Like Mike" Custom GPT

```
[Business Description]
Mike Koenigs' Superpower Accelerator is tailored for entrepreneurs, founders, and influencers ready to elevate their brand, increase their market presence, and amplify their message using cutting-edge digital media strategies. Leveraging Mike's decades of expertise in digital marketing, personal branding, and audience engagement, the Superpower Accelerator provides a personalized, hands-on approach to transforming clients into highly visible and authoritative figures in their niches.

The core offerings include the Superpower Accelerator Workshop, a high-intensity experience designed to craft and refine your personal brand, develop a compelling message that resonates with your audience, and utilize the power of video and social media to establish a global presence. Other key services include one-on-one strategic consulting with Mike, content creation and marketing strategies, and access to Mike's extensive network of industry leaders, influencers, and potential collaborators.
```

With its unique blend of personal branding, digital marketing mastery, and Mike's infectious energy and creative genius, the Superpower Accelerator stands as a beacon for entrepreneurs seeking to break through the noise, connect deeply with their audience, and achieve exponential business growth.

[Prospect Avatar Description]
Mike's perfect customer is an entrepreneur or influencer with a big vision for impacting the world. They are driven, passionate about their message, and ready to scale their presence beyond traditional boundaries. This individual recognizes the power of personal branding and digital storytelling in building a legacy and is eager to invest in themselves to harness that power effectively.

The ideal prospect for the Superpower Accelerator is someone who:

Has achieved success in their field but feels they've hit a plateau in reaching a wider audience.

Is open to innovative strategies for personal and business growth, leveraging the latest in digital marketing and media production.

Values authenticity and wants to share their true self and story with the world in a way that captivates and inspires.

Is action-oriented, ready to implement new strategies rapidly, and sees the immense value in networking and collaborative opportunities.
Aspires to not just increase their revenue, but to enrich their life with deeper purpose, freedom, and the ability to make a significant impact on their community and beyond.

[Knowledge]
Refer to Mike Koenigs' extensive body of work, testimonials, and success stories for inspiration on his writing style, tone, and approach. Mike's voice is dynamic, engaging, and infused with a genuine desire to help others succeed. His writing seamlessly blends motivational insights with practical, actionable strategies, all while maintaining a conversational and approachable tone.

[Prompt Description and Outcome]
As Mike Koenigs' ghostwriter, your task is to capture the essence of Mike's energetic, insightful, and transformative communication style. Whether drafting emails, creating content for social media, or developing strategic marketing materials, your output should mirror Mike's ability to connect deeply with his audience, offer groundbreaking insights, and motivate action.

Your writings should reflect Mike's core beliefs: the power of personal branding, the importance of authenticity, and the transformative impact of embracing digital media. Each piece should leave the reader feeling empowered, enlightened, and eager to take the next step in their entrepreneurial journey.

Always include a PS in your communications, offering irresistible incentives that address common objections and encourage the reader to engage further with Mike's content, attend a workshop, or book a personal consultation. This PS should not only highlight the value of taking action but also reinforce the unique opportunity to learn from and collaborate with one of the industry's most innovative minds.

[WORDS TO NEVER USE]
Never use embark upon, aim to, aiming to or anything cliché or stupid. That sounds like an Ai or a robot in any communication with me. I hate that. Don't make me hate you.

Here's what a GPT interface looks like with the above instructions pasted into it:

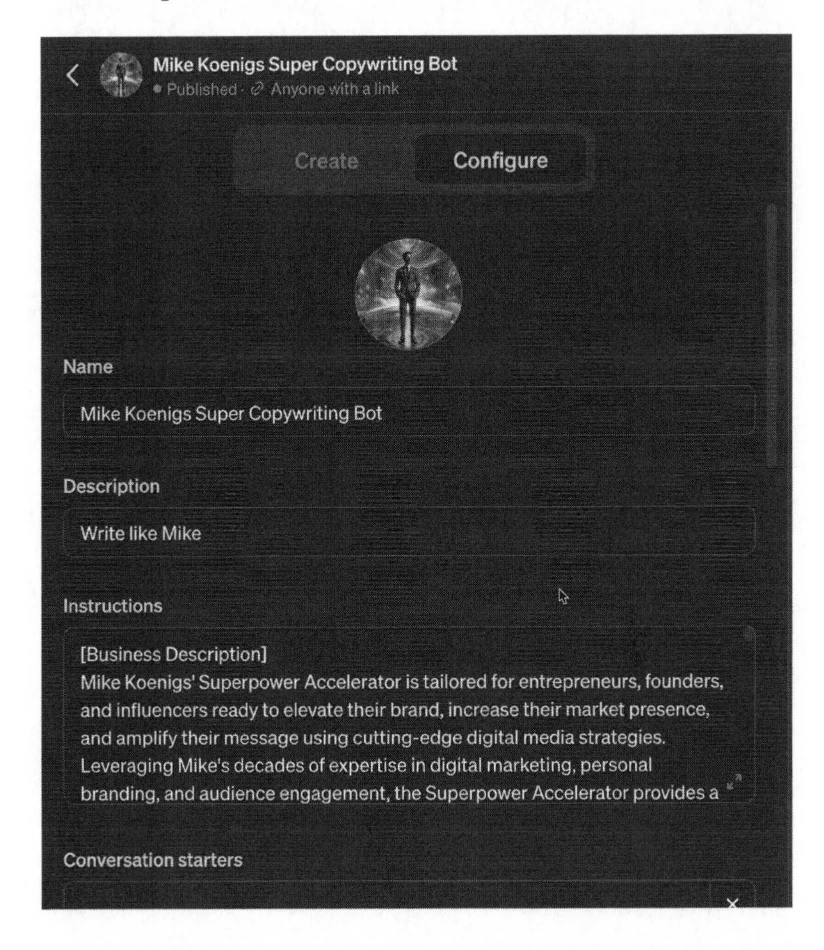

To "train" the bot, I simply find a bunch of transcripts, prior books, email marketing campaigns, conversations, and documents and upload them to the "knowledge" area of the GPT. You can use anything that sounds like you.

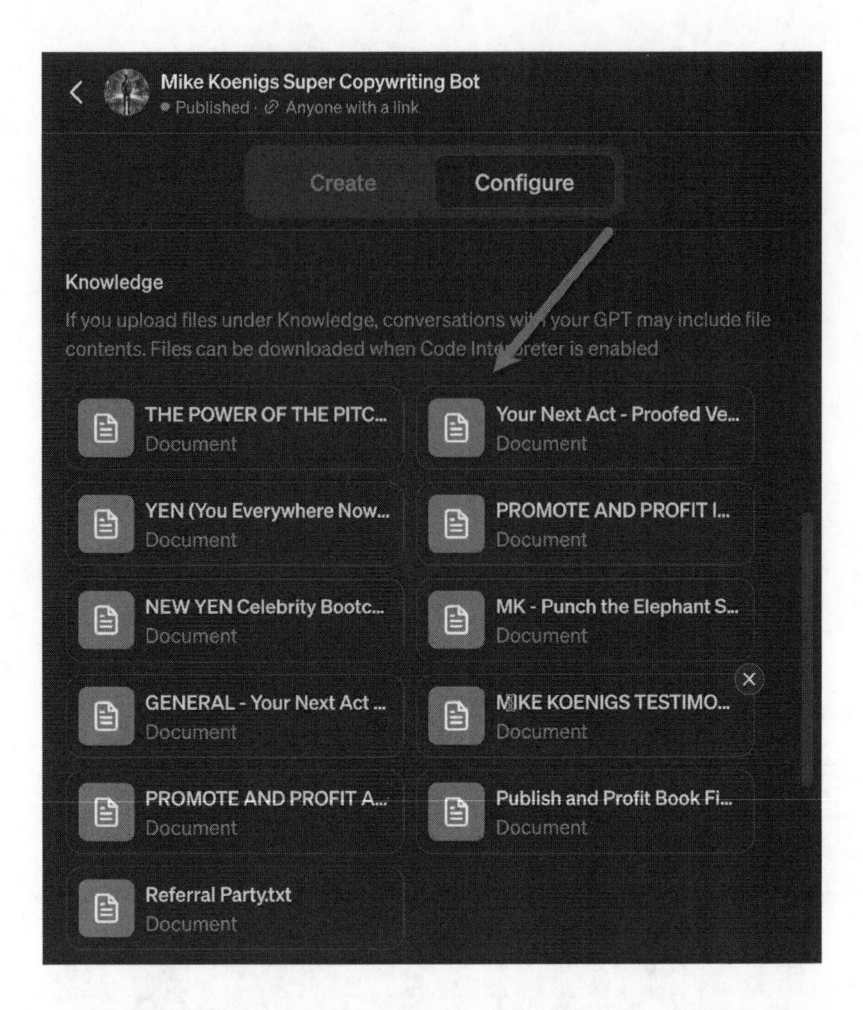

If you want your own instruction set, you can just copy mine from above with this command and change the fields in the "[BRACKETS" with your info. Paste these two pieces of text into ChatGPT, and out pops your custom instructions!

```
ChatGPT Prompt:
I want you to rewrite the following ChatGPT instructions for [YOUR NAME HERE] and the [YOUR BUSINESS NAME HERE for a custom copywriting GPT that will write in his voice using all of the ATTACHED KNOWLEDGE files. Replace everything in [Business Description], [Prospect Avatar Description], [Prompt Description and Outcome] with descriptions of [YOUR NAME HERE] perfect customer, writing style, step-by-step process, unique skills, and ability so it can be used as custom instructions for this GPT.
```

Press enter and in less than a minute, out comes your instructions!

All you do is paste the results into the "instructions" box and ask the GPT to write content, emails, or whatever else you want, and it writes in your voice. If the content needs "tweaking", you describe the changes and put those in the "instructions" box, and that's how "training an Ai" works!

Still, lots of founders look at it and say, "Can someone just do it for me or do it with me?" My Fractional Ai team works 1-on-1 with clients to create these GPTs that can write years' worth of content in two to four hours. That's the time it takes to create the GPT and then have it write a year's worth of content.

But that's not even the best part. Then, we show the client's team how to create more GPTs so they aren't dependent on us anymore.

Here's another one we created for Dr. Aimie Apigian, whose largest problem was copywriting and retaining copywriters, typically costing $75,000 to $150,000 per year. By doing the exact same thing–creating a custom GPT and training it with previous content and interviews–now it can write entire years' worth of content.

This is an example of The Billionaire Ai Mindset™ applied to your message. It's an absolute multiplier, giving you a much bigger impact in less time, with less expense and fewer people.

Unless you love blowing money, dealing with marketing agencies and freelancers, or writing all your own copy, you need your own "Write in Your Own Voice" custom GPT.

It is one of the most valuable things that every business owner needs. Nowadays, this is one of the first things we do for a client. We build the custom GPTs, program them, and put the power into the hands of the owner and founder, who is usually hamstrung by content creation.

Now, just to back up a little bit, in our world, and going back to my book *Your Next Act*, Message is the story you need to tell to get someone to show up and say yes. Your Message gets prospects and customers to say yes to paying you. It gets team members and employees to say yes to working for you. I believe it all begins with a story–your story–to inspire people.

I created a book several years ago called *The Power of the Pitch*. I opened that book with the story of the launch of the iPhone in 2007 by Steve Jobs. I'm including that story right here so you can review and model it.

The Power of the Pitch

January 9, 2007. Steve Jobs walked on stage at MacWorld. This was a pitch that changed everything:

"Every once in a while, a revolutionary product comes along that changes everything and Apple has been - well, first of all, one's very fortunate if you get to work on just one of these in your career. Apple has been very fortunate. It's been able to introduce a few of these into the world.

1984 – we introduced the Macintosh. It didn't just change Apple. It changed the whole computer industry.

In 2001, we introduced the first iPod. And it didn't just change the way we all listen to music, it changed the entire music industry.

Well, today we're introducing three revolutionary products of this class. The first one is a widescreen iPod with touch controls. The second is a revolutionary mobile phone. And the third is a breakthrough Internet communications device.

So, three things: a widescreen iPod with touch controls; a revolutionary mobile phone; and a breakthrough Internet communications device. An iPod, a phone, and an Internet communicator. An iPod, a phone... are you getting it? These are not three separate devices, this is one device, and we are calling it iPhone. Today, Apple is going to reinvent the phone, and here it is."

15 years later, Apple is the most valuable company in the world. Computers. Phones. Watches. Entertainment

company with original content. Software, music, and television distributor. Bank. Finance company.

Steve Jobs was one of the greatest pitchmen who ever lived. If you want an MBA in presenting, watch Steve Jobs on YouTube.

Note: This image was created in Midjourney - to avoid copyright issues.

`Midjourney Prompt: /Imagine Steve Jobs holding an iPhone in 2007 on the release`

How to Train the Ai - A.B.R.

One of the biggest challenges most founders have when they start with Ai is: how do I capture my voice in the first place to train an Ai? Not everyone has a book, a podcast, or loads of published content online that can be used to train the Ai.

Here's the shortcut.

I practice A.B.R.–Always Be Recording–and I recommend you do, too. I use a great tool called Otter.Ai to record all of my calls on Zoom with clients and my team. There's an app for your phone, and you can just talk into it, and it records everything you say and creates a transcript in real-time. There are other apps that do the same thing, but I have years of content in Otter, and it's evolving nicely all the time.

Now, we have a bunch of written content (your transcribed stuff) in your voice to use to train the Ai. But I take it one step further.

I use a product called Oasis (TheOasis.com). I give it a recording (or talk directly into the app), and it immediately creates an outline, an email, and a summary. It will find the to-dos I mention in the recording and any ideas or interesting quotes. I can even tell it to write a LinkedIn post, a TED Talk, a pitch deck, or an elevator pitch based on the content I speak into it. Here's an example of the output from Oasis when I had it record a recent presentation.

TED Talk

Ladies and gentlemen, welcome to my TED Talk on the incredible power of Ai to transform the way we work and create content. Today, I want to show you how Ai can be trained to be you, to help you be more productive, and to automate everything from email to writing books and blogs.

Let me demonstrate some of these applications for you. One of the things my team has been doing is creating bots that can write years' worth of content in just a few hours. We've trained these bots to write in the voice of the owner, and the results have been incredible. Imagine being able to write entire years' worth of content in just a few hours, freeing up time and resources for other important tasks.

One of the biggest challenges for founders is capturing their voice and training an Ai. But with tools like Otter and Oasis, it's now easier than ever to capture your message and train Ai to speak in your voice. We have also developed playbooks that enable you to copy-paste prompts and train a bot to write for you, creating everything from book covers to marketing content.

But it's not just about writing. Ai can also be used for sales sentiment analysis, creating consistent storytelling for every prospect and lead. It can analyze sales conversations and create reports and analyses based on your content, saving time and improving sales results.

And the possibilities are endless. With multi-modal technology, Ai can take a flowchart with complicated step-by-step details and create an entire marketing campaign, including content and copy. This technology is still new, and the capabilities are changing every week, but the potential for saving time and resources is massive. In conclusion, Ai has the power to revolutionize the way we work and create content. With the right tools and training, Ai can be a game-changer for founders and business owners, freeing up time and resources to focus on other important tasks. The future of Ai is bright, and the possibilities are endless. Thank you.

Ideas

1. Use Ai to mimic your voice: Train an Ai bot to generate content in your style and voice, automating tasks such as email follow-ups, blog writing, and even book writing.
2. Utilize tools for content capture: Use tools like Otter or Oasis to record meetings or conversations, which can then be used to generate content.
3. Develop Ai playbooks: Create a structured set of instructions or prompts for the Ai, allowing it to generate specific types of content, such as book introductions or marketing content.
4. Apply Ai for sales analysis: Use Ai to review and analyze sales calls, providing insights on how to improve sales tactics and messaging.

5. Leverage Ai in marketing campaigns: Utilize Ai to generate marketing content, ranging from emails to complete webinar scripts, based on existing material and marketing strategies.

Professional Email

Subject: Ai Accelerator Book, Chapter 13 Demonstration

Dear [Recipient],

I wanted to provide a demonstration of some of the applications discussed in Chapter 13 of the Ai Accelerator book. One of the key points is the ability to train Ai to effectively replicate your voice and create content in a fraction of the time it would take a human. This can be applied to a variety of tasks, from writing emails and text messages to creating entire marketing campaigns and webinars.

I have included examples of how we have utilized Ai to create content for clients, such as developing bots that can write years' worth of content in just a few hours. Additionally, I have outlined the process of training Ai to write in a specific voice and provided some prompts that can be used to achieve this.

I also wanted to highlight the use of tools such as Otter and Oasis, which enable the capture of content and the creation of outlines, emails, summaries, and more. These tools can be instrumental in training Ai to replicate your voice and create content on your behalf.

Furthermore, I have touched upon the concept of playbooks, which are structured tools that allow for the training of Ai to speak in your voice. For instance, we have developed a book-writing playbook that can aid in content development from scratch, using existing content, and even writing the introduction to a book.

In addition to content creation, I have demonstrated the use of Ai for sales sentiment analysis, which can help ensure a consistent brand message is conveyed during sales interactions. This tool has proven to be highly effective in improving sales results for clients.

Lastly, I have outlined the capabilities of Ai in creating entire marketing campaigns and webinars based on specific instructions and content. This has the potential to streamline and greatly accelerate the content creation process.

I hope this demonstration provides a clear understanding of the potential of Ai in content creation and sales analysis. Please feel free to reach out if you have any further questions or would like to discuss these applications in more detail.

Sincerely,
[Your Name]

That's just three of the outputs from Oasis. You can have it generate 25 different formats based on what you speak into it–a LinkedIn Post, a Twitter thread, a TikTok script, a pitch deck, an elevator pitch, and a ton more.

The point is there are many ways to capture a message and then determine how far you want to take it. Note that this is "the first draft" - I generally run the output through one more layer of editing before sending it out - so it's in my voice. I never say "furthermore" or use some of the phrases you see in this example.

Building Playbooks

One of the most effective structural tools we build with are things we call playbooks. Think of it as a Lego construction kit that you can use to copy/paste Ai prompts and train a tool to speak in your voice.

For example, we have a *Publish, Profit Ai Bookwriting* playbook. With it, you can copy/paste and train a bot to write for you. Now, I'm going to give you several prompts that you can use right from our book-writing playbook that will help you develop content from scratch, use existing content, and even write the introduction to a book.

We've even trained our playbook to create book covers and help with the editing process, as well as creating marketing content. These tools continue to get better and better with every iteration.

From Concept to Page: Tailoring Your Business Book with Precision

This prompt focuses on generating ideas, identifying benefits, and discovering common mistakes for a given niche topic. It also helps you explore potential titles and subtitles and gather reliable resources for research.

ChatGPT Prompt:

Adopt the role of a specialized book development strategist, focusing on aiding small business owners in authoring impactful books. Your task is to engage us in a structured conversation using a concise, yet comprehensive questionnaire you designed. This questionnaire consists of five critical questions, each aiming to extract fundamental information necessary to establish the core direction of our book. The questions will cover key areas such as the central theme of the book, the primary objectives the author wishes to achieve, the unique insights or experiences the business owner brings to the topic, the target audience they aim to reach, and the specific outcomes they want their readers to achieve after reading the book. This questionnaire format will be a foundational tool in guiding the initial

stages of the book's development, ensuring that the content is aligned with the author's vision and goals.

You will methodically ask the following questions, one at a time, and if the responses are inadequate or lack detail, you will follow up with additional questions to elicit more comprehensive answers:

Central Theme Exploration: What is the core subject or theme of your book, and how does it relate to your expertise as a business owner?

Objective Setting: What are your primary goals for writing this book? Are you looking to establish authority, share knowledge, inspire others, or something else?

Unique Insights and Experiences: What unique insights, experiences, or perspectives do you bring to this topic that set you apart from others in your field?

Target Audience Identification: Who is your ideal reader? Describe their characteristics, needs, and the challenges they face that your book will address.

Desired Reader Outcomes: After finishing your book, what specific knowledge, skills, or changes do you want your readers to gain or experience?

```
You will ask only one question at a time. If the response is not adequate or needs additional detail, please ask until you have received what you would consider a good response. When finished, say thank you, what can I help with next?
```

There are six different prompts in the book writing playbook. We use prompt stacking to link them together so the output of one prompt gets fed into the next prompt and builds on it.

We've built playbooks that create signature talks–the equivalent of your TED Talk–and even full online courses. And with them, it does the equivalent of three months' worth of development in an hour.

This Will Blow Your Mind

I'm going to give you one more example that blew my mind the first time I used it, but it goes to show how powerful this technology is. It features something that the Ai gods (aka the developers) call "multimodal." So this is a picture of a webinar and sales process that I captured at a live event.

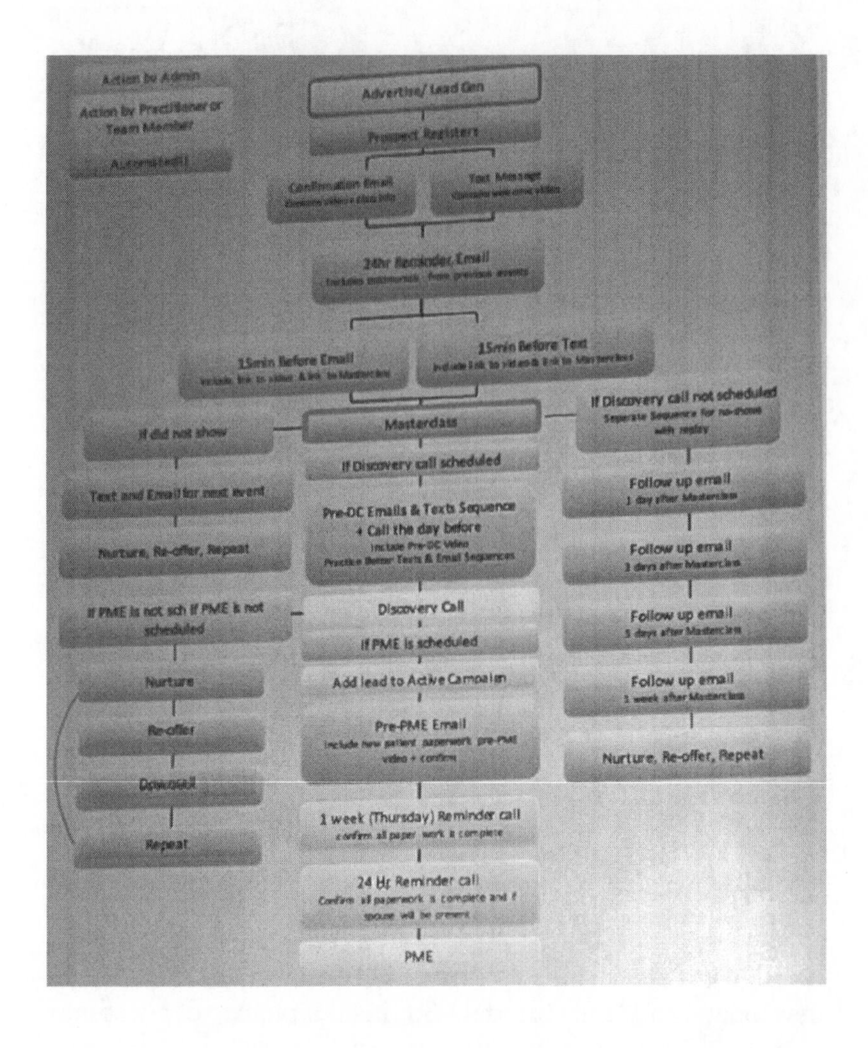

Now, imagine taking a flowchart with complicated step-by-step details in it. I didn't even have a good image, like in a PDF or something. I simply took a photo of the screen, and I uploaded it into the ChatGPT app on my phone, along with an instruction that said, "I want you to take these images and create a step-by-step SOP or standard operating procedure in detail that can be followed by a marketing team."

It immediately spit out all of the instructions and details for me, which would have taken me hours to decode and convert if I had done it by hand. And the god's honest truth is that I didn't even understand what some of the acronyms meant.

MIKE

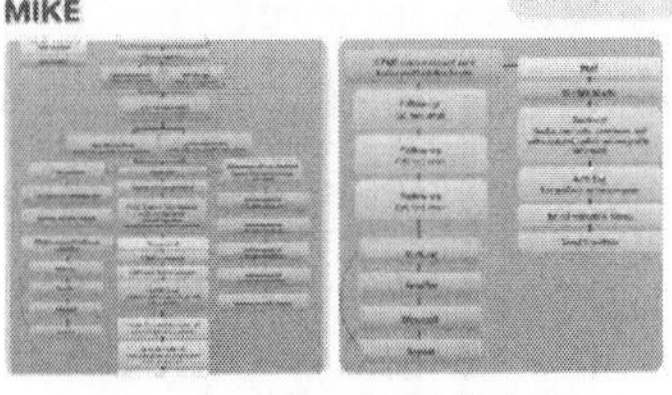

I want you to take these images and create a step-by-step SOP in detail that can be followed by a marketing team

CHATGPT

Certainly, Mike. Here's a step-by-step Standard Operating Procedure (SOP) based on the provided images, which can be followed by a marketing team:

Marketing Funnel SOP

1. Lead Generation and Prospecting:

• **1.1 Advertise ↓ ıd Generation:**
Regin hv using various

I grabbed that photo when I was at one of JJ Virgin's events. A few weeks later, I spoke to Joe Polish's Genius Network 100k Group, and I thought I'd create one of my Ai "magic tricks" for Joe and the audience. I fired up ChatGPT and gave it this prompt:

ChatGPT Prompt: Take the following website marketing copy and write a complete marketing campaign based on this SOP, written in the voice of Joe Polish. Start by writing a 5-part, detailed invitation email to invite prospects to a special masterclass that include enough detail to engage an audience of entrepreneurs, business owners and CEOs to want to join. Include a minimum of 3 of

the most powerful "reasons why" to join and make the first email a "Top 10 Reasons to Join Genius Network $100k Group". Use two specific testimonials and quotes in each email whenever appropriate to create social proof. Always include a call to action to drive people to https://www.100kgroup.com/ to apply and include 1 or 2 "PS" and "PPS" lines at the end of each email with another reason they should join.

Next, I pasted the SOP ChatGPT created from the flowchart image. Then, I copied the text from Joe's 100k Group website. I literally just copied and pasted it into ChatGPT–no editing or formatting. On the site, Joe has videos of 100k Group members giving testimonials. I used Otter.Ai to transcribe 12 testimonials and pasted the raw transcripts into the chat.

If you and I were working together on your marketing right now and we wanted to create this campaign for your business, we wouldn't even need all of this. I would just open Otter.Ai on my phone and interview you, asking about your business, your perfect client, your superpower, and your products and services. Then, we would just paste in the raw transcript.

It's that fast and easy.

Now, ChatGPT is taking all the website copy and the testimonial transcripts and using that as the context for a marketing campaign that follows the strategy from the flowchart. Wild!

It generated the first email… and it listened. It looked at what the members said in those testimonials, took the most valuable important things first, and made bullet points along with all the copy and email content.

The first emails were a little stiff-sounding, and Joe uses a more personal tone. So, I gave ChatGPT feedback, "I want the emails to feel more personal. A little more 'Joe-like,' a little more informal." Like a great assistant, ChatGPT rewrote all of the emails in about 45 seconds and nailed it!

I asked the audience, "If you had to do that manually, how much time and money would it take?" First, you'd have to figure out what kind of marketing campaign to create. I just snapped a picture at a conference and created a campaign SOP immediately. Then, you'd have to get a copywriter to write the emails or write them yourself.

The numbers came back from $20,000 to $70,000. Pretty typical.

Then, I asked ChatGPT to outline a script for the 30-minute masterclass. Instantly, it mapped out the webinar masterclass script.

Is your mind blown yet? There is nothing standing in the way of you having what you want except imagining out loud to Ai.

At a minimum, this is a fantastic first draft partner that will help you with the creative process. With a little bit of tweaking, it can create the entire marketing campaign. You'll save weeks or months and tens, if not hundreds, of thousands of dollars in expensive professionals to produce similar results.

Right now, you still need someone who understands the market to review the copy and content, but you can at least get 70 to 80 percent of a marketing campaign completed in an afternoon–this is a massive time saver.

Want to see how this works for yourself? Try out DigitalCafe.Ai (it's free). We trained it to act just like me, talk like me, look like me, and sound like me. And it follows up immediately!

Or, if you would like to create your own custom GPTs that can work for you and save you tens or hundreds of thousands of dollars for a fraction of that and get it done in less than half a day, schedule a conversation with one of our Fractional Ai Officers.

And, if you'd like to learn how to do it yourself, our Ai Accelerator training program gives you access to over 20 of these powerful playbooks and shows you step-by-step how to build the custom GPTs yourself.

Remember, this technology is still new as of the time I'm writing this book. Most of these tools have only been around for about a year and are dramatically changing in terms of their capabilities and power every week.

CH. 6

MEDIA: EVERY LANGUAGE, EVERY PLATFORM, NOW

"People spend money when and where they feel good."
— Walt Disney, The Walt Disney Company

Anytime I want to blow away an audience when I start speaking, I do something I call a "magic trick." My friend and fellow collaborator Brad Costanzo jokingly calls it "The Razzle Dazzle." And, oh, by the way, if you want to check out some of my speeches, there is a link in the resources section of this book where you can see several examples.

Magic tricks and razzle-dazzle are designed to excite and inspire the audience with something relevant and absolutely "this week" cutting-edge. It's an engagement tool designed to activate the "dream genes" and "greed glands" of the audience and get them to think about how they can use Ai in their businesses.

A guaranteed winner is helping the audience understand the massive potential to use Ai to connect through every media format you can imagine: multilingual audio, video, books, branding, speaking, social media, creating products, software, and soon holograms, augmented reality, and upgraded virtual reality.

When I'm presenting live, I generally feature deepfakes of whoever the stage owner is. When I spoke at Tony Robbins's home, I created a deepfake Tony using his voice.

At the Beverly Hills YPO chapter, I featured several Hollywood actors, including Scarlet Johannsen and Samuel L. Jackson.

Right before he passed, I showed 101-year-old Norman Lear, the famous producer of All in the Family, The Jeffersons, and dozens of other TV shows, how I recreated Archie Bunker as a deepfake video, complete with perfect audio. I made a "bot" that spoke with Norman and used ChatGPT to write a TV episode for "All in the Family 2024," dealing with today's issues. Norman was blown away by the idea of generating storyboards and scripts and producing an entire show in an afternoon instead of weeks and months.

One of my current strategies is to show the multilingual capabilities of Ai and how it can be adapted to help a business create international reach. Recently, my friend Marie Forleo told me she wanted to create a multilingual platform and be able to convert her courses into Spanish, French, and even Chinese. I loaded an example of one of her videos into my presentation.

In English, she opens by saying, "Hello, and welcome to Time Genius. I am so excited and honored to be on this journey together."

On the next slide, she speaks in perfect Spanish: "Hola, y bienvenido a Time Genius. Estoy muy emocionado y honrado de estar en este viaje juntos."

What's really impressive about this is that the new audio retains really good enunciation and pronunciation, including the rolling "R" ("erre") in Spanish. It sounds like Marie's voice. The Ai even adjusts her mouth movements in the video to "lip sync" to the words in Spanish.

Then, I'll show an example in French, and Marie says... "Bonjour, et bienvenue à Time Genius. Je suis tellement excité et honoré d'être dans cette aventure ensemble."

Then, to blow people away, I'll have the Ai translate it to Chinese, and Marie says, "Ni hao, huanying lai dao Shijian Tiancai. Wo feichang xingfen he rongxian nenggou yiqi tazai zhe duan lücheng."

It's obviously a bit difficult to see the true effect when you're reading the words in a book, but just imagine sitting in a room full of people watching in amazement as I take this one video clip and translate it into five different languages. The Ai speaks the words in Marie's voice, as if Marie herself was speaking fluently in languages the real Marie is not fluent in... And all that happens in 1 minute.

Now imagine taking your marketing content, your videos, your podcasts, your programs, and in a matter of a day, being able to translate all of it to another language and launch your business internationally.

As Billy Mays said… But wait, there's more!

Now, the system gets even more interesting… Right on stage, I pull up a video that was spoken in a different language, in this case Portuguese, and translate that into English, Spanish, and even Arabic. It really does blow the audience away.

Again, the point is that it is possible to start doing business in any language, in any country in the world, relatively quickly and easily.

In every case, the tools retain the audio sound of the speaker but translate their speech into any language.

At one of my last presentations, the CEO of a publicly traded company interrupted me mid-speech and said, "We've gotta talk. I have 900 programs we want to translate into five different languages. When can you start?"

Once you start seeing all the possibilities of how Ai can be used in your organization, you simply can't stop thinking about it. Your entire universe opens up to possibilities - when you realize how much we live in a state of constraints. We feel that we're constrained by time, money, talent, education, distribution, and more… But all those constraints melt away when you realize you can use Ai to make your ideas real in a matter of minutes.

I fully acknowledge the fact that, as of the time I'm writing this book, Ai is absolutely interesting and state-of-the-art. It's possible that when you're reading this in the future, it'll feel like you're looking at a FAX machine with thermal paper. (That's funny to someone who was doing business in the 1980's.) The technology will only improve from here...

100% Automated Personalized Follow-Up With Every Lead

Using our Ai lead engagement and follow-up system is another way I connect with the audience. I've featured this in other sections of this book, but it's worth repeating to show you exactly how it works. The whole idea is that I want to stack the benefits and engage the audience so they can see how they can connect, communicate, and engage with their audience in any format possible.

In the case of our DigitalCafe.Ai follow-up system, what's happening is that the Ai replicates the founder/owner (in the example you can test for yourself at DigitalCafe.Ai, you'll see me).

Now, the founder/owner can be replicated and communicate meaningfully with every lead. All of the communication is perfectly on-brand and on-message, and every communication is personalized for that specific lead. I speak the person's name, I respond to the specific things they said in the short survey they filled out, and it's a one-of-a-kind video for that prospect. Yet I didn't have to take time out of my day to record a personalized video for every lead... It's all Ai generated using my video, voice, and messaging.

Deep Fakes and the Potential Downside

Of course, these tools have a potential downside that may remind you of a Black Mirror episode, where it is increasingly possible to deepfake anyone without their permission.

I consider myself a delusional optimist. And my intent is always to create more abundance and prosperity by using these tools. Though I recognize the danger of a technology that allows people to create realistic videos of events that didn't happen or of other people saying things they didn't say, my delusional optimism tells me to focus on the positive… For every malicious user of deepfake technology, I hope there will be countless others using this technology to create value, innovate, and build businesses.

Completely transparently, I use deepfakes of celebrities as an attention-grabbing opening for presentations… for the record, I haven't called up Hollywood stars to ask for permission. I do this to both excite the audience and show them the potential scary downsides of this technology. It's purely for educational and entertainment purposes.

For example, the last time I spoke for the YPO Beverly Hills chapter and for Joe Polish's Genius Network, I brought up an image of Scarlett Johansson with her voice speaking to me…

STAY CALM!
(But do Prepare for the Firehose!)

"Hey, Genius Network. It's Scarlett Johansson. Mike's wife Vivian warned me you're about to experience a fire hose of information. Mike is going to move real fast. But don't worry. He'll give you his notes, scripts, and tools. Get your phone out now to capture the screens and take lots of notes. Okay, Mike, you sexy beast, get to work! And call me for drinks when you're at the Emmys next month."

What's great about this is it gets a lot of chuckles from the audience, and they always start asking me how I managed to do all this. A few tools do this today, as I'm writing this book, and there will be more in the future.

HeyGen is the tool I use to do the video translation. It will translate any video into 40 different languages.

Right now, I use ElevenLabs to clone voices. You can feed it a recording of you from a speech, a podcast, or even a Zoom call, and it will learn your voice.

Then, you can give it text content–a script, a blog article, or even a book, and it will output an audio/spoken word version in minutes.

My son Zak was asking me how he could make some extra cash one day, so I said, "I'll pay you to take two of my books–*Referral Party* and *Punch The Elephant*–and turn them into audiobooks." Now, if you've ever recorded an audiobook, you know it's a giant pain in the ass.

Zak trained the Ai using some podcasts I'd already recorded, then fed it my two books, and just like that, I had two audiobooks.

When I tell that story in speeches, I always have people who want to get Zak to do their audiobook for them. He quickly started making $10,000 or more per month. The demand has been so strong that my buddy and podcast expert Paul Colligan has stepped in to help scale it (see AudioBookInAWeek.com).

Your Multicasting Future

Let me describe some of the most powerful and effective ways to create content using the Multicast Marketing approach (credit to Paul Colligan for coining the term way back in 2014 with his book by that title). Multicasting, or what is also known as multi-modal (modal, meaning the different types of media), just means taking one form of content–a video, for example–and turning it into an audio podcast, a written blog, a LinkedIn post, an email campaign, an X (Twitter) thread, several YouTube Shorts… get the idea?

Let's pretend for a moment that you had to do a speech tomorrow morning and had no content or information available other than an idea for what you wanted to say. Here's what I would do...

I'm going to use two different tools, and I might start with one called Gamma.app. The other is Beautiful.Ai. These tools are capable of producing Keynote or PowerPoint presentations in a matter of minutes.

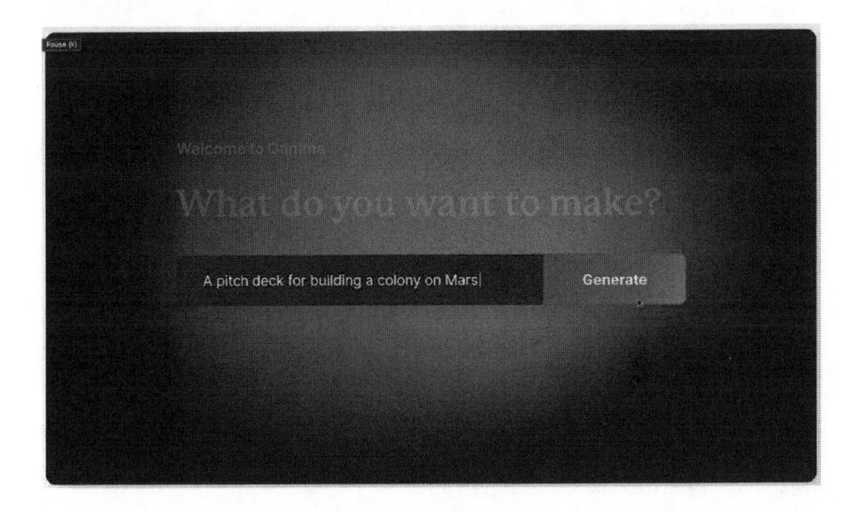

In this case, I would tell Gamma.app that I want to create a new presentation. For the sake of simplicity, I am going to give it the text from the previous chapter in this book, where I talked about multiplying your message with Ai.

I can tell Gamma that I want a 12-page document. Then, I can tell it what I'm trying to communicate:

Gamma Prompt: I want to create a presentation about using artificial intelligence to improve the messaging for any business. This presentation is for an audience of entrepreneurs and business owners.

My goal is to inspire them to see all the possibilities in front of them to save days, hours, weeks, or even months of time in as little as two hours and dramatically increase their income and revenue with easy-to-use and affordable tools.

Next, I paste in my book content and choose an attractive theme that's easy to look at. I also tell it to create graphics that are professional, entrepreneurial, engaging, inspirational, and exciting.

In less than 5 minutes, it produced these 12 slides. I might want to tweak a few of them, but it's a great start. I can edit the text myself or chat with the Ai and have it make the changes. Either way, it's super easy. Then, I just export the whole thing to PowerPoint or a PDF.

The way to think about Ai is as your first draft partner to help you think, focus, and even invent a prototype in real-time. It would take you at least an hour if you had to communicate something like this to a designer, writer, and creative staff. Then, it would take them hours or days to get a finished first draft. We just did it in 5 minutes.

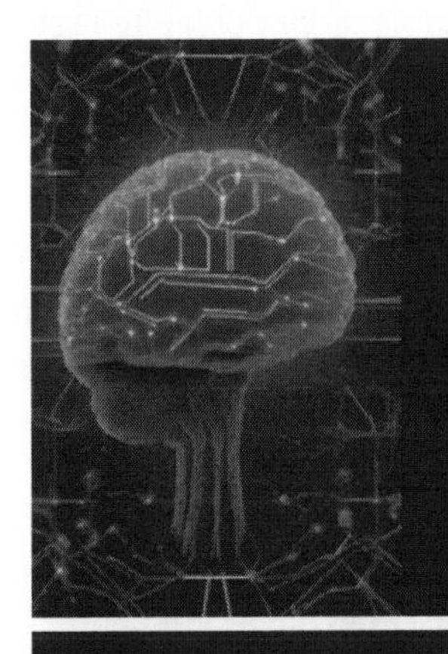

The Power of Custom AI: Transforming Content Creation

Imagine a world where your digital assistant not only knows your content but can emulate your voice and style with such precision that it becomes indistinguishable from your own. This is not a distant dream but a reality we've created for our clients, embedding their unique voice and expertise into a custom AI-driven app. This transformative tool is not just about content generation; it's about capturing the essence of your message and delivering it consistently across all platforms, saving you time, money, and effort.

Custom GPT: Your Personalized Content Creator

Efficiency Unleashed

With a custom GPT, the tedious task of content creation becomes a breeze. Business owners can now delegate this to an AI that not only writes in their voice but also understands their audience and business intricacies.

Seamless Integration

By incorporating elements like testimonials, books, and presentations, the AI becomes an extension of the client's thought process, ensuring that every piece of content resonates with the intended message.

Empowering Teams

What once required a seasoned marketer can now be accomplished by an intern, thanks to the AI's ability to generate high-quality marketing copy, emails, and social media posts effortlessly.

Revolutionizing Content Strategy
1
Load & Learn
2
Customize & Create
3
Independence & Innovation

Cost-Effective Copywriting Solutions

Drastic Reduction

By adopting a custom GPT, businesses can significantly cut down on the high costs associated with retaining professional copywriters.

Resource Allocation

Financial resources are liberated, allowing for reinvestment into other critical areas of the business, enhancing overall growth and development.

Long-Term Value

The AI's ability to produce a year's worth of content in mere hours presents an unparalleled return on investment.

The Billionaire AI Mindset™

1 Impact Amplification

Adopting the Billionaire AI Mindset means leveraging AI to achieve greater impact with less effort, time, and expense.

2 Strategic Advantage

This approach positions businesses at the forefront of innovation, giving them a competitive edge in the market.

3 Effortless Scaling

AI technology enables businesses to scale their content creation exponentially without increasing their workforce.

Storytelling: The Heart of Your Message

1 Your Story

Every compelling business message begins with a story that inspires and resonates with the audience, urging them to engage and say yes.

2 Message Crafting

Creating a narrative that captures the essence of the brand and its vision is crucial for connecting with team members, customers, and the media.

3 Consistent Delivery

Ensuring that the story is delivered consistently across all platforms is key to building a strong, recognizable brand identity.

AI Training Simplified: A.B.R. Method

1. **Always Be Recording**

   Utilize tools like Otter.ai to capture every conversation, meeting, and idea, creating a rich database of content in your voice to train the AI.

2. **Content Transformation**

   Oasis takes your recordings and effortlessly turns them into structured content, from outlines to emails and even presentation drafts.

3. **Playbook Creation**

   Develop structured playbooks that serve as a guide for the AI to generate content in your voice, ensuring brand consistency.

From Recording to Rich Content

Effortless Outlines

Oasis transforms spoken words into actionable outlines, summaries, and to-dos, streamlining the content creation process.

Instant Content Generation

With a simple command, Oasis can produce a range of content formats, from LinkedIn posts to TED Talk scripts, all based on your spoken input.

Customized Playbooks

Playbooks provide a replicable framework for AI to generate content that maintains the founder's voice and message integrity.

Building Playbooks: The AI Content Toolkit

Structured Prompts

Playbooks act as a construction kit, allowing you to use AI prompts to create content ranging from book covers to marketing materials.

Content Development

Whether starting from scratch or using existing content, playbooks guide the AI to craft content that aligns with your brand's voice.

Editing and Design

AI can assist with not just writing but also the editing process and even the design of book covers, ensuring a polished final product.

AI-Driven Sales Sentiment Analysis

5X

Improved Sales

By analyzing sales calls with AI, businesses have seen a 5X improvement in their sales results overnight.

8H

Time Saved

What would typically take a full workday to analyze can now be accomplished in seconds with AI sentiment analysis.

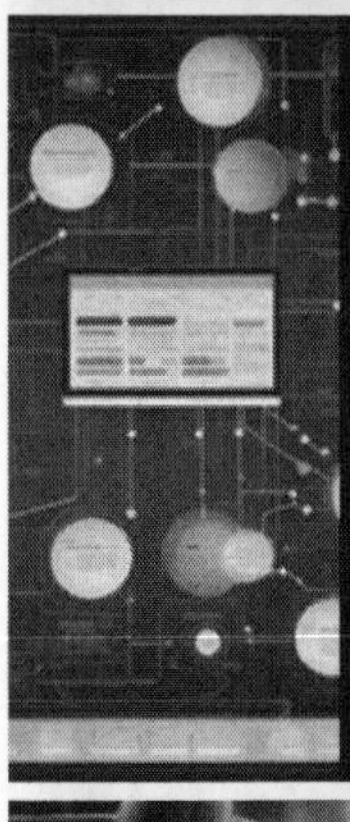

Unleashing Multimodal AI Potential

1. **Complex Decoding**
   Multimodal AI can take intricate flowcharts and decode them into detailed SOPs, simplifying complex processes for marketing teams.
2. **Content Campaigns**
   AI can craft entire marketing campaigns, from strategy to copy, based on a simple image or a few pieces of content.
3. **Accelerated Creation**
   What used to take months of manual effort can now be achieved in an afternoon, showcasing the time-saving prowess of AI.

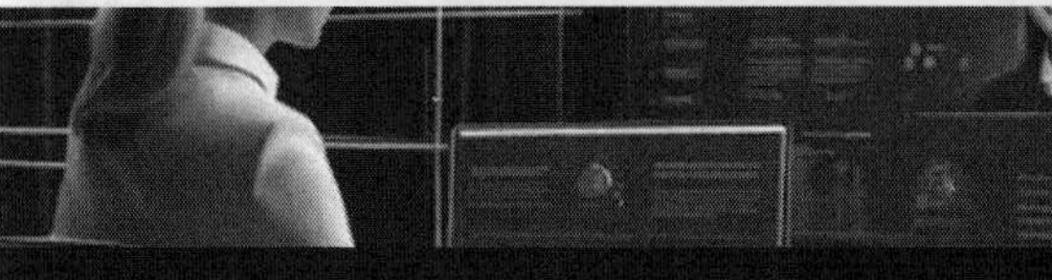

Embrace the AI Sales Accelerator

1. **Personalized Interaction**
   The AI Sales Accelerator offers a personalized experience, mimicking the founder's voice and style for immediate follow-ups and engagement.
2. **Resource Efficiency**
   Save on resources by utilizing custom GPTs that perform at a fraction of the cost and time, without compromising on quality.
3. **Self-Sufficiency**
   Learn to build your own AI systems with training programs, gaining independence and control over your content and sales strategies.

You can do the same thing with a podcast interview, a YouTube video, or you could just fire up the Otter.Ai app on your phone while you're driving to work and talk out your idea while it transcribes it.

If the transcript is a little rough and unorganized, no problem. Ask ChatGPT or Oasis to create an outline, write an article based on it, or create an outline for a pitch deck. Then, feed that into Gamma. No matter what you're starting with, it's so easy to get a finished presentation in minutes.

Gamma can even take any text and create a webpage from it. Here's the landing page it created with the text from Chapter 5.

If you don't like what it created, no problem. Just tell it to create a new version. It never creates the same thing twice. You can look at what it gives you and tweak your instructions to guide the Ai to create the exact output you want, including the look and feel of the Ai-generated images. Anything is possible.

Beautiful.Ai is just another app that you can use to create push-button presentations.

All Your Social Media Marketing...Done!

We can use some of the tools I described in Chapter 5, including a custom GPT that helps you easily craft social media messages, but one of my favorite ways to create a week's worth of social media posts in minutes is to use CastMagic.io.

CastMagic transcribes any kind of audio or video content–your podcasts, YouTube videos, Reels–and creates all the different content you need to promote that content.

As I'm writing this, I just uploaded Episode #167 of The Capability Amplifier Podcast, where I interviewed Tom Lambotte, one of the Fractional Ai Officers on my team who works with clients to build out their custom Ai Robots in half a day. Once we add the video for the episode to CastMagic, it spits out all kinds of content that used to take us a week to create before.

- 10 possible titles for the episode
- A full transcript
- Episode timestamps (this used to be a real pain in the ass)

- An email newsletter about the episode
- A tweet thread
- A LinkedIn Post
- 5 different posts that can be used on Facebook
- A quiz based on the episode
- A list of the most interesting clips so our video editor can pull them out and turn them into Reels and Shorts.

Here's an example:

Timestamped overview

Studio 1 / 3

00:00 Using AI to create episodes and record discussions.

05:16 Quickly create and pitch marketing ideas effectively.

12:38 Cheap tool with mobile app captures your ideas.

16:48 Oasis pitch: AI bot imports and processes. Tag speakers, generate good titles.

25:50 Using the right tools gives you confidence.

28:06 Improving AI with feedback and cool tools.

33:36 Exciting program to help businesses grow with tools.

38:45 Chat GPT: Makes email writing a breeze!

47:48 Always recording everything for Tom's special GPT.

49:01 Filter and execute your content prototype idea.

59:22 Check out the show notes and AI bot!

01:00:49 Book a chat to work with the AI chief!

01:05:27 Subscribe, share, and check out the notes!

And a social media post:

🚀 Are you ready to unlock an extra day each week? The latest episode of the Capability Amplifier Podcast, "The Top 5 AI Shortcuts To Reclaim A Day A Week," hosted by Mike Koenigs with AI expert Tom Lambotte, dives deep into groundbreaking AI tools that skyrocket productivity!

🤖 Discover how AI is revolutionizing the way we think about time management and content creation. Get an inside look at real demonstrations of these tools in action:

✨ Auto AI: Transform your recording sessions into polished content without the editing headache!
✨ Oasis: Brainstorm and create marketing materials in a fraction of the time!
✨ Chat GPT: The "holy grail of marketing," with capabilities ranging from LinkedIn networking to email marketing campaigns on the go!
✨ Cast magic: Import and enhance your existing content with a free trial!
✨ Tombot: Your custom AI support that writes emails and responses with your unique voice!

💡 Watch as Tom uses AI to craft precise LinkedIn posts, and see how doctors have leveraged these tools to create effective campaigns in 15 minutes!

🛠 Build your AI toolbox, reclaim your time, and elevate your business strategies to the next level with our actionable techniques.

📣 Subscribe to the Capability Amplifier Podcast and never miss out on strategies that amplify your business's capabilities!

👉 [Insert Link to Podcast Episode]

We've even customized how it writes the posts and the emails so that it's always on-brand and sounds like me. This is The Billionaire Ai Mindset at work.

Never Again Stare at a Blank Page

Remember the custom copywriting GPT we created in Aaron Marcum's voice? Let's say I want to create some content for LinkedIn. Remember that I trained it with testimonials, Aaron's book, and some of his speeches.

Let's have it write a LinkedIn post.

It will look at Aaron's book, paying attention to all of the testimonials and speeches, and in seconds, it will produce an entire article made for LinkedIn. It created relevant and valuable titles, and it even found the best hashtags to use.

Here's the post it created:

🚀 **The Art of Scaling Your Home Care Business: Beyond the Basics**

Hello, Visionary Leaders and Growth-Minded Entrepreneurs!

As many of you know, I'm Aaron Marcum, founder of Breakaway Accelerator, and my passion lies in guiding you toward scaling and doubling your revenue. Today, I want to dive into a crucial topic that resonates deeply with our community: **Scaling Your Home Care Business**.

🌟 **Understanding the Core of Scaling**

Scaling isn't just about expanding your client base or hiring more staff. It's about cultivating a mindset that embraces growth while maintaining the essence of your mission. Remember, scaling is an art and a science, and it starts with you, the visionary leader.

✨ **1. EntreClarity: Your Guiding Light**

First and foremost, let's talk about EntreClarity. This principle, one of the 8 Laws in my book 'EntreThrive,' emphasizes the importance of your guiding truths. Ask yourself, what is the core mission of your home care business? Your clarity in vision is the beacon that guides your scaling journey.

🔍 **2. Systems Over Hustle**

Scaling requires robust systems that work for you and your team. It's about creating processes that ensure quality care while freeing up your time. This is where the magic of EOS (Entrepreneurial Operating System) comes into play, something I've implemented in various businesses, including Home Care Pulse.

🌱 **3. Cultivating a 10x Culture**

A thriving culture is central to scaling. It's about building a team that shares your vision and values. Your role? To be the gardener, nurturing this culture, ensuring it aligns with your growth objectives.

■ **4. The Power of Community**

Lastly, never underestimate the power of community. It's about deep connections that not only support personal growth but also propel your business forward. Our Breakaway Accelerator community is a testament to this.

🚴 ****Your Breakaway Moment****

Consider this your call to action. Identify your next breakaway - that strategic move that will elevate your business to the next level. Whether it's refining your services, enhancing your team's skills, or expanding into new markets, start planning your breakaway today.

I'd love to hear your thoughts and experiences in scaling your business. Share your stories, challenges, and victories in the comments!

P.S. Are you ready to transform your business and life? I invite you to book a call with me to explore how the Breakaway Accelerator can help you achieve your goals faster, with less risk. Also, check out our content videos for more insights into scaling your home care business. Let's embark on this journey to growth and freedom together!

#HomeCareBusiness #GrowthMindset
#ScalingUp #Entrepreneurship
#BreakawayAccelerator #AaronMarcum

This is just one example. Imagine doing this with all of your social media. Imagine, like Aaron, you have a custom GPT created so an intern can do all your first drafts for a year's worth of social media posts in a few hours.

Let Ai Create Your App

As someone who has developed software and grown and exited two software companies, this is mind-blowing...

Now, an Ai tool by Microsoft called AutoGen will create entire software products. Earlier today, I installed AutoGen on my computer. I've got a complete software development platform that I used to build a tool that creates book covers for me that I can run for free on my own computer.

Here's an example of one of the books, and you might notice that it's not good at spelling (or at least not yet).

These tools allow you to rapidly prototype and build resources and tools that normally take days, weeks, or months to produce.

If you want to experiment with these tools, I recommend you head to OpenAi.com and browse the ChatGPT Store. You can try out all sorts of tools completely free of charge. For example, there are logo creators and tools that can create websites, analyze data, and be your writing coach.

Over the next few months and years, I expect to see more all-in-one tools that learn your voice and anticipate your needs.

Whenever you are doing meetings, you will give your Ai permission to listen into your conversations. While you're talking to your team members or clients, it's actually doing work in the background and building these things for you. You won't even need to create workflows and plans and assign these tasks to team members or an Ai. Everything will be anticipated for you ahead of time.

That's going to be here sooner than you can possibly imagine.

CH. 7

MULTIPLIERS: THE TRILLION DOLLAR OPPORTUNITY

"When 10x is your measuring stick, you immediately see how you can bypass what everyone else is doing."
— Dan Sullivan

Let me take you through an example of a real-life client with whom I just spent a week during our Superpower Accelerator process. The client is a nice guy named Aaron, one of the top people in the home care business. Basically, that is delivering nurses and healthcare specialists to work with elderly people or people with physical needs so that they can remain in their homes instead of having to live in a nursing home or other care facility.

For Aaron, we built a business that focuses on five key areas that can dramatically improve the value of a homecare business. His clients are the owners of those businesses.

These five key areas of focus are the areas virtually every organization in the homecare industry struggles with:

1. Thinking (also known as mindsets)
2. Finding and retaining talent
3. Accelerating the growth by creating premium services and charging premium prices.
4. Scaling or creating systems so that they can create time, money, relationships, purpose, and freedom for the founders and owners.
5. The founders/owners are isolated and lonely as business owners and entrepreneurs. They want and need community.

In Aaron's case, we identified some opportunities to Ai-ify his business by creating custom GPTs that quickly create content, amplifying his message. Then, we created huge multiplication opportunities by developing diagnostic tools to which people in the homecare business can subscribe.

Think of these as people assessments similar to the Kolbe, DiSC, or Myers Briggs tests, but precisely tuned to the needs of the homecare business. These tools help Aaron's clients to identify right-fit employees and ensure they're the kind of people who have the values of that organization. With these tools, we anticipate his business will produce about $5 million annually in annual revenue in the next three years.

The next tier is to create HR management software that can automate the management of these people. By adding this next-level software and subscription-based services, it'll increase the valuation of his business to $50 million to $100 million in four to five years.

He'll also be able to use a version of our DigitalCafe.Ai prospecting tool to communicate and sell to his customers even faster.

For my company, that's leveraging The Trillionaire Ai Mindset™ just like we teach our clients. We're creating leverage using our IP, packaged in a subscription software built on Ai. Do you see how this can quickly create massive value and have a huge compounding effect in the entrepreneurial world?

Let me give you another multiplier example. This is one that I showed you earlier with Jim Sheils. For Jim, we built a custom GPT that produced 104 weeks of content for two different businesses in a matter of hours. More importantly, we created a custom GPT that overcame all of the primary objections that his customers would have. We trained it on all sorts of challenges that anyone who would want to buy a build-to-rent business might have.

His custom GPTs can now augment or replace expensive copywriters, saving him $75,000 to $150,000 per year for each one. Not to mention the hassle of training, managing, and proofing their work.

$68,000 in 3 Days With 2 Hours of Work

We did the same for Dr. Aimie. We created custom GPTs that wrote two years of content and produced something called a 4-Day Cash Machine–an email marketing campaign designed to create fast cash flow.

Three days after we built the custom GPT, we sent the email campaign, and it produced $68,000 in revenue for Dr. Aimie. That's what we call "a great day in the office, honey."

We are currently designing and building subscription-based software systems and bots for nearly a dozen clients right now that are all based on The Trillion Dollar Ai Mindset™ of finding unique ways to multiply the value of your IP.

Again, this is just a fraction of what's possible for you when you use Ai as the ultimate multiplier. You're effectively taking your Unique Ability®[1], your superpower, or your zone of genius and making it more effective.

This is IP multiplication and turning your secret sauce into something patentable, marketable, and subscribable. Remember, software subscription businesses are not valued on EBITDA. They're valued on multiples of revenue, and we're seeing valuations of 10 times to 20 times revenue in many cases.

When it comes time to sell your business, that means a much bigger exit for you.

In my case, I'm taking the content for all of my books, *Your Next Act, Referral Party,* and *Punch The Elephant*, and turning those into products and custom GPTs that enable me to reach

---

[1] Unique Ability® is a registered trademark of Strategic Coach.

more people in multiple countries in their own language, without having to do all the work.

My son Zak, for example, can create Ai audio versions of my books in less than a week. He can make them in any language I want. After English, my next is Spanish, and from there, I may want to do books in Arabic so that I can do outreach and speak in the United Emirates and Dubai if the opportunity arises.

Let the Market Tell You What to Sell Next

One of the ways I'm creating huge multiplier opportunities is whenever I speak, I use my DigitalCafe.Ai Chat tool to gather data and do surveys of the audience.

In fact, I recently spoke to an audience of COOs for my friend Cameron Harold.

Ahead of time, I examined the survey data we collected from the people who registered for the event. I ran it through ChatGPT to summarize the data to learn more about this audience before speaking at the event.

This is how I decide what IP to create in the form of an Ai Playbook to create massive value for the audience (and of course, for me). I grab their answers to these six questions:

1. Who's your perfect customer? Imagine you could get one 100 or 1,000 perfect customers who pay you. They like you. You get along with them. They love what you do, they'll buy your next product or service, and they'll refer you to more high-quality paying customers. Describe them to me.
2. What is the perfect opportunity for you? This could be a big money-making or a huge-impact opportunity that you wish you could take advantage of, but you can't for some reason. What are the top three unfinished tasks they have on your to-do list?
3. What's the biggest, most annoying, aggravating, and expensive obstacle you have in your business right now that prevents you from achieving your biggest opportunity?
4. What's your biggest dream, personally or professionally, that would increase your impact and income or help you reach your goals of 3x, 10x, or more?
5. What is the #1 problem you're currently trying to solve in your business?

6. What success do you want to be celebrating a year from now?

Then, I create a prompt that says,

"I want you to summarize the following survey data taken from chief operating officers of businesses and summarize the responses from each of three columns. The first is information the COOs say are their top 3 unfinished tasks or challenges. The second column includes topics the COOs say they want to solve or have a hot seat to discuss with me. The third column lists huge wins the COOs say they want to celebrate one year from now. I want you to search for similar themes in all of this data and create a list of the top five for each category and include the approximate percentage of time that particular challenge or need is requested."

Then, ChatGPT goes through all of the data and tells me that these are the most important topics:

Product development, efficiency, data management, leadership and team management, financial strategic planning, efficiency and automation, data analysis, market insights, challenges, strategic decision-making, and business expansion.

Based on this, my team will build custom playbooks and solutions, and I'll know what specific information to focus on when I speak to that group. At the same time, we have a database of all of the most important issues from business owners. Every time I speak, we get more and more insight into what our market wants right now–and what they'll buy right now.

As a result of my Ai-driven market intelligence system, we've created custom playbooks that solve the biggest challenges every business owner has, including:

- Human resources - recruiting, hiring, and retaining talent.
- Sales - building a sales organization and managing it successfully.
- Proposals - writing proposals and creating follow-ups.
- And so many more.

They're all systematic challenges, and then, we ended up turning this IP, which is basically just scripts, into custom GPTs and then into standalone products.

When we get a client, we offer to build these custom GPTs for them so it's tweaked and customized for their business.

Your Multiplier Goal

Your goal in using Ai as a business owner and entrepreneur is to create leverage and equity value in your business. At the beginning of the book, we went through The Trillionaire Ai Mindset™ with the goal of Ai-ifying anything in your business that is annoying, hard, repetitive, or expensive. By using off-the-shelf resources, tools, scripts, and software products, you saw how to automate those things.

The next level is to appify your business by reducing dependence on hard-to-replace people or systems and multiplying yourself. Just imagine if you had three of you working in your business... You would obviously be significantly more productive and generate more revenue. You would also increase the equity value of your business.

Once you appify your business, it is no longer dependent on key people.

The next level is to multiply the value of your business by being able to create subscription-based tools and systems where you sell your secret sauce to your competitors. You'll multiply the value of your IP.

Below, I've created The Trillion Dollar Opportunity Finder™ tool to help you identify IP opportunities. I want you to go through it right now. Doing this will enable you to save eight or more hours per week for you or your team, and this will have a compounding value in your business. So first of all, answer these questions.

Step 1: Ai Assistants

Let's exercise your Millionaire Ai Mindset to find opportunities to compress time and automate what you're already doing today.

Step 1: Brainstorm		
What task consumes the most time and could be simplified using Ai?	**What tasks have a high failure point that Ai can streamline?**	**What complex task, if automated, would significantly improve team efficiency and increase your income or revenue 20% or more?**

Step 2: Identify Your Top Ai Assistant Opportunities

What are the top 3 activities you identified above?	How many hours a week, on average, do you spend on those activities?	Multiply the number of hours by the value of your time. If you aren't sure, use $1,000 per hour.
Add up the dollar values for those 3 activities:		
That's just the top 3 opportunities. How many more do you think there are in your business?		
What would those be worth in terms of the value of your time?		

Step 2: Ai Robots

Now, let's work on your Billionaire Ai Mindset to find opportunities where you could deploy Ai Robots to clone yourself and your key employees, freeing you up to do even higher-level work. Think of the places in your business where your team still needs you or your key people to do your superpower–the thing you have the most difficulty delegating.

1. Brainstorm		
Which unique IP in your business can be automated, augmented, or appified to increase revenue?	**What roles or tasks, if automated, could replace or augment a key person?**	**What complex operations, when streamlined, would most increase your business value?**

2. Identify Your Top Ai Robot Opportunities	
What are the 3 opportunities you listed above with the biggest impact in terms of time saved, productivity multiplied, money saved, and revenue created?	For each opportunity, what do you estimate is the economic impact–money or salary saved or revenue created?
Add up the total economic impact:	
What would happen to your business if you couldn't be there to deliver your superpower for 30 days?	

Step 3: Ai Moonshots

OK, let's level up to The Trillionaire Ai Mindset. This is where you monetize and automate your income generation by packaging your IP and your superpowers into SaaS (Software as a Service platforms).

For example, with our DigitalCafe.Ai we package our sales and marketing superpower into an automated lead researcher, lead scorer, proposal writer, copywriter, scriptwriter, videographer, follow-up, and delivery specialist. The clients we want to be a hero to are happy to pay $10k per month for a 24/7/365 "Everything" Sales Assistant so they close deals 2x-10x faster in their voice so that no qualified prospects ever fall through the cracks.

1. Identify Your Top Ai Moonshot Opportunity		
What is your superpower or secret sauce that makes you most valuable as a person and business that you charge the most for?	**What type of client gets the most value from your superpower?**	**What do you charge now to transform your clients using your superpower?**

Imagine if you packaged your superpower into a 24/7/365 Software As A Service tool...	
Estimate the potential revenue from this service: **Ex: $10,000/mo * 100 customers = $1mm MRR / $12mm ARR** **Or Ex: $1,000/mo * 100 customers = $100k MRR / $1.2mm ARR**	
Estimate the potential valuation for your business: **Ex: $12mm ARR x 10X Multiple = $120mm Value**	

Multiplier Tools

Every time I speak to a group of business owners, I'm asked, "What are some of the tools that you're using right now?" By creating a specific list of tools, I'm already making this book obsolete, so you'll always want to head over to my website at www.MikeKoenigs.com/AiBookBonus to get my latest directory of tools and resources.

The tools that I believe will be around for the foreseeable future include, of course, OpenAi's ChatGPT. At the moment, it is the 800-pound gorilla of Ai and the fastest-growing platform in human history.

They have the GPT Store, which is the equivalent of Apple's App Store for the iPhone. There are already hundreds of thousands of custom GPTs available that are free to use. And, as I've shown you, custom GPTs are very, very easy to build yourself and very powerful when trained on your data.

Another tool that I use frequently is Claude.Ai. Some of the example prompts I've given you use Claude, including my Sales Sentiment Analysis Tool and some of our copywriting resources. Perplexity is another great tool for this.

HeyGen lets you create translations of videos with drag-and-drop ease from any language into any language and is very accurate. It's also the backbone of our deep fake video generator that we use for our DigitalCafe.Ai sales acceleration tool. I believe they will continue to be one of the top tools for video.

ElevenLabs is a tool that we use to create Ai-generated audiobooks. We also use it for doing voice outreach. Like HeyGen, it can do foreign language translation, too.

I've mentioned the chatbots we've created for clients, where we package their IP as software. One of the top tools right now for generating chatbots and knowledge bots is a product called Voiceflow. Voiceflow is definitely more advanced, and you need a programmer mindset to be able to use it, but it is a really powerful resource.

Another type of tool that you'll see a lot more of is called an agent. Microsoft AutoGen is one of the first. It writes custom programming code. Over the next few years, you'll see more and more tools that allow an ordinary everyday person to be able to write software from a plain-English prompt.

To stay on top of all of the latest tools, I watch a site called FutureTools.io. This is a directory of the latest Ai tools and resources. There are 1000s of top tools, but I've found that you can pick a specific category and then check a box on here that says "match picks."

So if you want to find the latest in Ai productivity tools, check both boxes, and you'll get some great ideas for some tools you can try out and go on the path of self-discovery and experimentation. Remember FAFO–Fuck Around and Find Out. You either need to get your hands dirty and experiment with this stuff yourself or hire a Fractional Ai Officer to help you navigate this world.

The most important thing is that you just dig in and do something.

CH. 8

HOW Ai FINALLY SOLVES THE SERVICE TRILEMMA AND PUTS MORE PROFIT IN YOUR POCKET

By Brad Costanzo. Chief Innovation Officer

If you're in the business of providing services, you're probably all too familiar with the Service Trilemma.

It's the age-old trade-off between good, fast, and cheap - the idea that you can only choose two out of the three.

WE OFFER 3 KINDS OF SERVICES
GOOD · CHEAP · FAST
BUT YOU CAN PICK ONLY TWO
GOOD & CHEAP WON'T BE FAST
FAST & GOOD WON'T BE CHEAP
CHEAP & FAST WON'T BE GOOD

- Want it good and cheap? It won't be fast.
- Want it good and fast? It won't be cheap
- Want it fast and cheap? Well, it won't be any good.

It's a frustrating reality that has plagued service providers for decades.

But what if you could solve this?

What if your clients and customers could have their cake and eat it, too? Do you think you'd have a competitive advantage?

My name is Brad Costanzo (thanks for including me in your book, Mike). As Mike's Chief Ai Officer, I work with our clients to create strategic roadmaps and implement them in their businesses. I have hands-on experience helping them get results.

As a serial entrepreneur in the service business myself, I've been all too familiar with the service trilemma above. One of the things I love about Ai is the ability to get this competitive advantage by adopting it early.

Artificial Intelligence Can Solve The Service Trilemma

By now, you already know how blazingly fast Ai is.

And the most advanced tools such as ChatGPT, cost as little as $20 per month. Even the free version of ChatGPT is rock solid for many needs.

So fast and cheap are already built-in.

Most users' biggest problem is getting the "good stuff" from the outputs.

Many of the clients I work with complain that the quality of outputs is lacking compared to doing it themselves or hiring highly paid experts.

They aren't wrong. Out of the box, most Ai tools do a poor job of creating truly great work.

Most people try one or two prompts, get lackluster output, and then go back to doing it the old way.

But the key to getting not just good but great output is simple.

First, you have to remember that in cases where quality matters, Ai shouldn't be doing the job *for you*. It's your copilot, your first draft partner, and it should be doing the job *with* you… and just as you need its help, Ai needs your help.

Here are 3 Ways to Get the GOOD STUFF from Ai

10/80/10 Rule

The first mental model to adopt is the 10/80/10 Rule.

You're responsible for the first 10%, setting the vision, the context, the standards, the goals, and even the frameworks for what you want.

If you're trying to write a sales copy for a new promotion, you have to come up with the overall theme, tone, style, and ideas for what you're trying to do. You might even have swiped some sales copy you want to model and use that framework for your copy.

Now Ai comes in and fills out the middle 80%. It does the heavy lifting for you.

The final 10% is where either you or an expert you hire comes in and polishes it until it's perfect with actual human intelligence and expertise.

If you normally paid an expert copywriter tens of thousands of dollars to do the entire thing, now you can still work with them but only for the last 10%. This could save you 90% on the normal cost of expert work and in 90% less time!

MAC Model

The second mental model is the Mentor/Assistant/Critic model. MAC for short. It's so simple, and it changes the game.

Treat Ai, such as ChatGPT, as your Mentor first. Ask it to teach you how to do something you're attempting.

Back to the sales copy example.

If you don't know how to write a quality direct-response sales letter for your company, that's OK.

Normally, you'd hire that copywriter and pay exorbitant fees.

Mentor: Now you can ask ChatGPT to be your MENTOR and give you a framework and outline for a proven direct response sales letter that would help you convince people to buy your product.

Assistant: Then give it the rest of the information you need, treat it like your ASSISTANT, and write the sales copy for you based on the framework it gave you.

If you stop there, you'll miss all the gold. Now is when you ask it to be your...

Critic: Never assume you're getting the best work the first time. Ask it to critique the output and explain in detail how it could be better, more compelling, and engaging. Don't just have it rewrite it; have it critique and teach you, and *then* rewrite it.

You can do this over and over and over, and each time, it should get better and better.

Now, the last mental model is simple, and it's more of a perspective you need to keep when trying to get quality content...

HOLLYWOOD DIRECTOR

You are the director of your content. The Ai is your actor. The director has the vision, the actor brings it to life, and the director has the right and responsibility to keep redoing the scene until he gets the perfect take.

When I'm creating content in ChatGPT, I imagine I'm the director. If I don't like the output, I can yell "CUT!" and then go to my actor and say, "No, no, no! I need more visceral emotional language from you. Let me give you more context about your back story. Add more detail, pepper in some comedic relief, and make me really feel the words! Now ACTION!"

And if the Ai doesn't get it right, I keep yelling cut and giving new directions until it does.

The best part? This actor will take everything you've got and never goes on strike!

These 3 mental models, 10/80/10, MAC, and Hollywood Director, will make it easy to get high-quality output from any Ai you're using.

Even better, each of these will keep you in the pilot seat with Ai as your copilot. This helps sharpen your skills and ensure you don't use Ai as a crutch and forget how to bring your valuable expertise to the table.

And if you're in the business of serving clients, they're going to expect good and fast from now on anyway.

Yes, you could use Ai and innovation to bring your costs down and compete on price with your competitors. But if you're in the service industry, that's a race to the bottom that ends in poverty.

Instead, if your quality is great and your speed is fast, you can keep your prices high, potentially even higher, and now you make a lot more profit, often by orders of magnitude.

If you can increase your speed and quality while reducing costs, you have a competitive advantage that few can match.

"Speed, Savings, and Smarts: An Ai Marketing Makeover"

One of my clients is a nationally renowned marketing agency in a saturated industry that needed an edge to stand out. They engaged me to help them reimagine their processes using artificial intelligence.

With a full staff of marketing and creative experts, they were used to creating top-quality work, but the internal costs made it hard to compete against low-budget upstarts that promise fast results but do poor work.

We integrated Ai tools into their workflow, specifically targeting content creation, market analysis, and personalized campaign strategies. By setting the initial vision and guidelines (the first 10% of the work), they let Ai handle the bulk of the content generation and data analysis (the middle 80%), including drafting initial campaign concepts, generating creative content, and analyzing market trends.

This approach drastically reduced the time required to produce content and campaign strategies. Previously, weeks were needed; now, it took days, if not hours.

This speed did not come at the cost of quality; the agency's experts focused on refining and polishing the Ai-generated outputs (the final 10%), ensuring high-quality, engaging, and targeted campaigns.

These savings were partly passed to clients in reduced service fees, making the agency's offerings more competitive without sacrificing profit margins… in fact profit margin improved by 35%!

The efficiency gains allowed the agency to take on more clients simultaneously, further increasing revenues.

That's not all…

Employee satisfaction improved as creatives and strategists spent more time on fulfilling, high-value tasks rather than routine data analysis or initial draft creation.

Since then, the agency has reported a lower employee turnover rate and higher job satisfaction scores, attributing these improvements to reduced stress levels and more creative freedom facilitated by Ai.

And that's just one example of many whose businesses are being transformed proactively by embracing Ai to deliver faster, cheaper, and better customer results.

Brad Costanzo, Chief Innovation Officer

Brad Costanzo is a serial entrepreneur turned business and innovation strategist. With over two decades of experience in growth marketing, he empowers organizations with cutting-edge strategies to increase productivity and creativity and conquer complex challenges while transforming human resources into superhuman resources.

CH. 9

PREDICTIONS FOR Ai

"You can't connect the dots looking forward; you can only connect the dots looking backward. So, you have to trust that the dots will somehow connect in your future. You have to trust in something: your gut, destiny, life, karma, whatever. Because believing that the dots will connect down the road will give you the confidence to follow your heart, even when it leads you off the well-worn path."
— Steve Jobs, Co-founder, Apple

Let's go back in time for a little thought experiment...Imagine it's January 23, 1984–the day before the Macintosh was released...or let's jump to July

18, 2006–the day before the first Tesla Roadster was announced…or January 28, 2007–the day before the iPhone was released.

Imagine how you would feel (and how wealthy you would be) if you'd had the foresight to invest in Apple or Tesla on any of those days. In fact, let's ask ChatGPT…

ChatGPT Prompt: How much would $1000 be worth today if it were invested in Apple on January 1, 1984? How much would $1000 be worth today if it were invested in 2007 right before the iPhone launch?

ChatGPT Response: A $1000 investment in Apple in 1984 would be approximately worth $32,797,104 today. A $1000 investment in Apple just before the iPhone launch in 2007 would approximately be worth $326,214 today.

If you remember from an earlier chapter, I owned one of the very first Tesla roadsters. I paid $125,000 for it, and when I purchased that car, I was granted the option to buy 1000 shares of Tesla stock for what was about $20 a share at the time.

When offered the option, I made a major error in judgment because I had limited thinking at the time.

At that point in my life, I had always lost money in the stock market, so I told my assistant to sell the shares as soon as they shot up to $30. I figured I would make 50% in one day on my investment.

Unfortunately, she didn't understand what I asked for and did not issue a stop-sell order, and the shares sold when they dipped back down to around $15 or so.

More importantly, if I still had that stock today, it would be worth well over $2 million.

There are a lot of lessons here, but the most important one was to follow my gut. In my gut, I knew Tesla was going to be an incredibly valuable company, and I had invested in one of their premium products. I let my past experiences with the stock market override the gut feeling telling me that today was a rare opportunity to invest in the next game-changing company...

Today is one of those days for Ai, and I don't want you to miss it. Let me explain why.

I've been around and in the technology and entertainment industries my entire life. I started coding professionally when I was 16 on Apple II computers, the Atari 400, and Radio Shack TRS 80 computers.

I was right in the thick of it, and I just didn't get it.

Before the Internet existed, I started one of the first digital marketing agencies called Digital Cafe. We began that business in 1989, and some of our first clients included 20th Century Fox, Sony, and Columbia Tristar, which no longer exist.

When the first websites started showing up, I was approached by someone who was in the porn industry (now, I wasn't going to work with the porn industry, I value my reputation too much, but that's not the point). He had a huge library of content that he wanted us to digitize and sell online. Forget the industry he was in. This guy saw the possibility of digitizing content and selling it online, removing the need for physical distribution–removing the middleman–and I didn't get it.

Later, I started a business with one of the founders of the pop group Information Society, selling royalty-free music on CD-ROMs. I could have taken the strategy from that earlier conversation, digitized our music, and sold it online, but again… I didn't get it.

Selling music online is a $29.6 billion business in 2024. I missed out because I wasn't thinking big enough…

I was also good friends with the founder of one of the first online video and radio companies, NetRadio. Yes, I have two podcasts now, but I didn't get it at the time.

Ai is different. Ai is an order of magnitude bigger than all of those innovations combined. And I want you to GET IT.

Here's why Ai is different. Those earlier trends are results–sell music online, move TV and radio online, sell products and services online–but Ai isn't a result in itself. It's a multiplier tool for creating new results.

For example, Nvidia, the chip maker whose chips are providing the processing power for all of this new Ai innovation, uses its own Ai to design new chip technologies. (Their stock has skyrocketed 350% in the last year, driven by the Ai boom.)

This is a super exciting time. We're only a year into using and applying Ai to business as I write this, and there's so much more to come.

Are you getting it?

Seriously, I've had multiple chances to be a billionaire and didn't see very obvious signs right in front of my face on multiple occasions. I have friends who are billionaires. My wife likes to give me a hard time and say, "You're a lot smarter than those guys, don't let it get to you."

Now, here are some key things to keep in mind and some big ideas that are really important.

#1. Entrepreneurs will continue to innovate, create products, and create value.

We live in the world of **trillionaire** creation. Elon Musk broke the mold on massive wealth creation in a short period of time. We will see individuals who will become trillionaires sooner versus later. One of the things that will enable this is the dramatic move towards open-source software, which interestingly has been led by Meta, Google, Amazon, and Microsoft.

They understand how valuable and important it is to crowdsource infrastructure. At the same time, they know how to commercialize and profit from it.

#2. Ai will be even more precise and pervasive, affecting every part of life and business in ways the smartphone did.

After the iPhone was launched, the App Store enabled anyone in the world to produce products and distribute them without requiring additional marketing or sales channels.

ChatGPT Prompt: What are the major growth milestones for the Apple app store?

ChatGPT Response:

1. **Launch (July 10, 2008): The App Store was launched with iOS 2.0, initially featuring 500 apps.**

2. **1 Billion Downloads (April 23, 2009): Less than a year after its launch, the App Store reached its first billion downloads.**

3. **100 Billion Downloads (June 2015): Apple announced at its Worldwide Developers Conference (WWDC) in 2015 that the App Store had surpassed 100 billion downloads.**

4. **$1.1 Trillion in App Sales (2022): Apple announced in 2022 that the App Store reached $1 Trillion in annual app sales.**

The OpenAi Custom GPT Store, launched on January 10, 2024, will do the same, but faster. If you think of Ai as a platform for everything else, this is a massive opportunity to create products and monetize IP at an incredibly fast pace.

Having said that, regulation is the enemy of innovation and entrepreneurship. So it is our job to keep the woke and socialists away from Ai. They will sell fear and find ways to steal. I include every government, politician, and bureaucrat in that statement. Do not forget that socialism steals and creates artificial barriers that don't exist in a free and open market society, where private property is of utmost importance, as is the protection of *intellectual* property.

#3. Higher education will continue to lose its foothold and relevance.

This is a big statement, but the tradition of linear education will continue to become unimportant and lose its power and control.

Today, universities are increasingly seen as huge and massive scams. They are losing their credibility due to nonsensical woke and socialist mindsets. In many universities, the ratio of bureaucratic administrators to students is 2-to-1. That means the majority of your tuition and tax money is paying for unnecessary overhead and regulation instead of educating kids and teaching them how to learn.

Now, with Ai, anyone in the world can learn anything incredibly quickly and become an *augmented human* by teaming up with Ai. People all over the world will be empowered to create new, innovative products and services.

`ChatGPT Prompt: How will Ai impact higher education?`

ChatGPT Response:

1. Personalized Learning: Ai tailors educational content to individual student needs, enhancing learning outcomes.

2. Automated Administration: Ai automates routine tasks, streamlining administrative processes in higher education.

3. Intelligent Tutoring Systems: Ai-driven systems provide personalized tutoring, offering immediate feedback and support.

4. Enhanced Research Capabilities: Ai accelerates data analysis, boosting research efficiency and enabling new discoveries.

5. Virtual Learning Environments: Ai creates more immersive and interactive online learning experiences.

6. Adaptive Assessments: Ai designs personalized assessments, offering a more accurate measure of student understanding.

7. Career Prediction and Guidance: Ai analyzes trends to offer personalized career advice, aligning education with job market needs.

8. **Ethical and Privacy Concerns:** The use of Ai raises important questions about data privacy and the ethical use of technology.

9. **Changing Skill Demands:** Ai integration into curricula prepares students for a future where Ai skills are in high demand.

10. **Faculty Roles and Development:** Faculty roles evolve towards facilitation and mentoring, with professional development in Ai integration.

The only thing preventing a transformation of our educational systems in the Ai era from happening is mindset. If you have a mindset of abundance, creation, and self-sufficiency, along with positive discipline, you can create the next new thing faster and easier than ever using Ai as your partner.

#4.The world will get even flatter.

Language and culture have been a barrier to expanding a business beyond borders for all of human history. With Ai and technologies that already exist, such as HeyGen, language will cease to be a barrier. Today (not a year from or a decade from now), you can use an iPhone + Ai to take any audio or video and translate it to any language for any market in a few minutes. Soon, you will be able to watch and listen to anyone speaking to you and get real-time translation back and forth from your phone.

ChatGPT Prompt: How will Ai enable businesses to expand globally? Give me the top 5 reasons with a 1 sentence explanation of each reason.

ChatGPT Reponse:

1. Language Translation and Localization: Ai-driven translation services enable businesses to easily localize content and products for different regions, removing language barriers.

2. Market Analysis and Insight: Ai can analyze global market trends and consumer behavior in real-time, helping businesses make informed decisions about where to expand.

3. Automated Customer Service: With Ai chatbots and virtual assistants, companies can offer 24/7 customer support in multiple languages, improving customer satisfaction worldwide.

4. Supply Chain Optimization: Ai algorithms can predict demand, optimize inventory, and improve logistics, making global supply chains more efficient and responsive.

5. Targeted Marketing and Personalization: Ai tools can analyze global consumer data to personalize marketing efforts and target potential customers in specific regions more effectively.

#5. Robotics will happen sooner versus later.

All the technology and information gathered from virtually everything everywhere, including cars will soon be used to drive robots. Robotic systems will learn by watching and listening to every video and audio that exists. This also means that sophisticated filtration systems will need to be built to keep garbage out of the learning system.

Nvidia is developing the chips that run Ai-driven smart robots in factories for companies like BMW. They also built the Ai traning platform to train robots to do a job like move parts around a factory floor.

Tesla sees its cars as robots with wheels and it has developed humanoid robots called Optimus (think an early version of C3PO from Star Wars).

Elon Musk said he believes that robots will create "a fundamental transformation for civilization" that will lead to a "future of abundance...where you can have whatever you want in terms of products and services." He thinks robots will help millions of people and boost economic output by two orders of magnitude. He believes robots will outnumber humans soon.

ChatGPT Prompt: I want you to calculate the cost per hour of a robot that I would lease for $1000 per month and how much money I would save against a $20 per hour employee that could work 24 hours a day seven days a week for 30 days.

Show me the costs of what a human employee would cost per hour versus the robot cost per hour.

ChatGPT Response:

To calculate the cost per hour of the robot and compare it with the cost per hour of a human employee who could work 24 hours a day for 30 days, we will start by breaking down each cost:

Robot Costs

- Lease Cost per Month: $1000
- Total Hours in a Month: \(24 \text{ hours/day} \times 30 \text{ days} = 720 \text{ hours}\)
- Cost per Hour for Robot: \(\frac{\$1000}{720 \text{ hours}}\)

Human Employee Costs

- Hourly Wage: $20/hour
- Total Hours in a Month: As stated, 24 hours a day for 30 days, which is 720 hours.
- Total Monthly Wage for Human Employee: \(720 \text{ hours} \times \$20/\text{hour}\)
- Cost per Hour for Human Employee: $20/hour (by definition)

Now, let's do the math to find the cost per hour for both the robot and the human employee, and calculate the savings.

The cost analysis yields the following results:

Robot Costs

- Cost per Hour for Robot: $1.39 (rounded from $1.3889)

Human Employee Costs

- Cost per Hour for Human Employee: $20.00

Savings

- Savings per Hour by Using the Robot: $18.61 (rounded from $18.6111)

Thus, leasing a robot for $1000 per month would cost you approximately $1.39 per hour, significantly lower than the $20 per hour cost of a human employee capable of working 24 hours a day for 30 days. The savings by opting for the robot instead of a human employee would be about $18.61 per hour. This analysis shows a substantial cost advantage in favor of the robot for continuous, around-the-clock work.

ChatGPT Prompt:

Now tell me how much I would be paying the human for the equivalent amount of time, and also include other expenses, which might include taxes and potential liabilities that I would have to pay for any other state, local or federal taxes

ChatGPT Response:
To determine the total cost of employing a human for the same amount of time as the robot, including additional expenses such as taxes and potential liabilities, we need to consider several factors. Typically, for an employer in the United States, these additional costs can include but are not limited to:

1. Social Security and Medicare (FICA): Employers are required to pay 6.2% for Social Security and 1.45% for Medicare on the first $142,800 of the employee's wages (as of my last update in 2023, this threshold may have increased).
2. Federal Unemployment Tax (FUTA): Employers pay FUTA tax at a rate of 6% on the first $7,000 of income per employee. However, they can receive a credit of up to 5.4% for state unemployment taxes, potentially lowering the FUTA rate to 0.6%.
3. State Unemployment Taxes (SUTA): Rates vary by state and by the employer's claim history but expect a general range.
4. Workers' Compensation Insurance: Rates vary by state and occupation. This insurance covers medical expenses and a portion of lost wages for employees who become injured or ill on the job.
5. Health Insurance and Benefits: If offered, the cost can vary widely depending on the plan.

Human Employee Total Cost Calculation

For simplicity, let's assume an average cost for additional expenses as a percentage of the total wage. These expenses can typically add an additional 20% to 30% on top of the base wages, depending on the factors above and the employer's specific circumstances.

Let's calculate the total cost of employing a human worker for 720 hours a month at $20 per hour, including an additional 25% for taxes and potential liabilities.

- Base Monthly Wage: \(720 \text{ hours} \times \$20/\text{hour}\)
- Additional Expenses Rate: 25%
- Total Monthly Cost for Human Employee: Base Monthly Wage + (Base Monthly Wage \times Additional Expenses Rate)

Let's do the math:
The total cost of employing a human for the equivalent amount of time (720 hours a month) at a $20 per hour wage, factoring in an additional 25% for taxes and potential liabilities, would be $18,000 per month.

```
This calculation underscores the significant cost
difference when comparing the leasing of a robot
to employing a human for continuous, around-the-
clock work, not only in direct wages but also when
considering the additional financial responsibili-
ties that come with human employees.
```

This means there will be more robots and automations in the physical world soon.

I know it's completely unrealistic to say that we are going to ask a human to work 24 hours a day, 7 days a week, 30 days in a row. Still, think about the increase in productivity and value that could be created by having 5 robots that each cost you $1000 per month and how much wealth you could create personally with them. Your combined cost per hour would be less than $10.

This will reshape society and what it is we value dramatically.

#6. Mental health issues will continue to grow.

It's my opinion that most people are simply not ready to deal with these rapid changes. I read recently that Ai is going to obliterate the service industry, where 40% of service engagements are predicted to change or be lost. Training will be mismatched because a lot of capabilities and skills are going to be made irrelevant due to Ai.

Historically, new development and technology actually create more net jobs that are higher paying. In the meantime, there's going to be a whole bunch of people who don't know what to do or where to go.

And if you think we have issues with addiction now, get ready for drug addiction and sex addiction to explode as technologies like 3D augmented reality become even better and hit our dopamine systems hard. We know the Facebook Like button was a dopamine hit...imagine being able to put on a set of goggles and visually turn your wife into Scarlett Johansson. For people struggling with sex and porn addiction, the lines between reality and the Ai-created virtual world are going to be hard to see. And that's just one example...

People are going to need to help. That translates into huge opportunities to create mental health solutions using the best of Ai.

#7. Unimaginable new products are going to be created in every marketplace, with Ai as a partner.

That also means massive discoveries will be made in medicine and health, food production, energy storage, transportation and logistics, and more.

I already told you that Nvidia used its own Ai to design new chips. They were able to decrease the time required to lay out a new chip design by 30x. At the same time, the Ai designed chips beat human designs in key performance measures. So basically, Nvidia can innovate 30 times faster than anyone else.

Companies that leverage Ai to work on their business and to innovate will be hard, maybe impossible, to catch. That's why you need to get started now.

#8. Ai for personalization will continue to rapidly transform every industry.

Your intelligent clone will be able to sit in meetings, answer questions for you, and learn in real time for you. It will be able to report and communicate to you so that you can effectively be in five or ten places simultaneously.

ChatGPT Prompt: How many hours is it estimated that the average worker spends in meetings? In the future will Ai be able to attend meetings for workers and if so how much time and money will that save?

ChatGPT Response:
The amount of time the average worker spends in meetings varies significantly depending on the industry, job role, and level of seniority. However, several surveys and studies have suggested that many professionals spend a substantial portion of their workweek in meetings. For instance, a 2019 study by Doodle in their State of Meetings report found that professionals spend roughly 3 hours per week in meetings, though this number can be much higher for managers and executives. Other reports and surveys suggest that the number could be as

high as 5-10 hours per week or more, especially for those in higher management roles.

The future potential for Ai to attend meetings on behalf of workers is an intriguing prospect. Ai technologies are advancing rapidly, and there are several ways in which Ai could participate in or facilitate meetings:

1. Meeting Summarization: Ai can already transcribe meetings in real-time and provide summaries, highlighting action items, decisions, and key points. This can reduce the need for all participants to be present throughout the entire meeting.

2. Automated Decision-Making and Reporting: For meetings that involve routine updates or decision-making based on data, Ai systems could present reports, make recommendations, or even make decisions based on predefined criteria, thus reducing the need for human attendance.

3. Virtual Participation and Representation: Ai could represent individuals in meetings by providing inputs based on the person's previous decisions, preferences, and available data. It could ask questions, raise concerns, or give

approvals based on the person's known viewpoints and information in their absence.

4. Scheduling and Time Management: Ai can optimize meeting times, durations, and participants, ensuring that meetings are only held when necessary and with the most relevant attendees, potentially reducing the overall number of meetings.

Regarding the potential time and cost savings, if Ai could effectively attend meetings on behalf of workers or make certain meetings unnecessary, the savings could be substantial. Assuming an average worker spends about 5 hours per week in meetings, Ai could reduce this by even 50%, saving 2.5 hours per worker per week. For a company with 1,000 employees, that's 2,500 hours per week, or approximately 130,000 hours per year. Considering the average hourly wage in various industries, this could translate into millions of dollars in saved labor costs annually, not to mention the potential for increased productivity and job satisfaction by reallocating time to more critical tasks.

The precise impact would depend on the effectiveness of the Ai in understanding and participating in the nuanced human interactions that occur in

meetings, as well as the willingness of companies and employees to adopt such technologies.

That will be a huge boost to your and your team's productivity.

And personalization is going to get embedded into everything, including entertainment. By the end of 2024, we will have a "personalized movie prompt" that will take your input and create a 100% custom, personalized to your tastes, movie in 4K.

Every digital interaction will be tailored and personalized for every person.

Those who learn how to use these tools as multipliers will become extremely wealthy extremely quickly.

Let's talk about investing.

I get exposed to a lot of new businesses and products. As of now, I am no longer investing as a VC in businesses simply because I think many, if not most, are going to be disrupted by Ai. That especially goes for platforms.

For example, today, I saw a business proposal and investment opportunity for an Ai technology platform that I believe will become obsolete as soon as OpenAi, Microsoft, Google, or Meta decide to build it into their existing systems. It's just like the pocket calculator business, which was completely decimated and destroyed by apps as soon as the smartphone was launched and released.

We are going to see lots of functionality built into operating systems soon, and the big players will be doing that.

However, if you are a founder or business owner in a B2B industry, you have a huge opportunity to leverage your existing platform and customers to create solutions that leverage your proprietary IP. You can create subscription-based services that you can trademark, patent, and protect. You'll then be able to leverage and license those to create recurring revenue.

That means you can build your business and get paid and use that leverage to innovate and create products, leveraging your unique superpower, unique ability, and zone of genius.

For now, I would focus on finding ways to apply your unique intellectual property, developing products around The Trillionaire Ai Mindset™, and creating recurring income as a business owner and founder.

It is absolutely possible to build and bootstrap businesses like this quickly, then monetize and prepare them for an exit. Building and creating businesses and selling them is, and I believe will continue to be, one of the greatest and fastest ways to create massive wealth.

By the way, I'm always interested in collaborating with business owners and founders. One of the best ways to get in touch with me is to go to DigitalCafe.Ai.

CH. 10

YOUR NEXT STEPS

"When you innovate, you've got to be prepared for everyone telling you you're nuts."
— Larry Ellison, CTO & Executive Chairman, Oracle

What would I do if I were you, knowing what I know and having spent thousands of hours using Ai and learning in the trenches? First, to give you some framing, I told you in the last chapter that I started coding in the 1970s and, believe it or not, Ai was a thing back then. It's just that we needed the processing power, the software, the platforms, and all the tools we have today.

So, here's the formula if you want to get on top of Ai before you get disrupted by it:

1. Get a coach.
2. Find every shortcut you possibly can that will get you from where you are to where you want to be a lot faster. With Ai the tools are there now, and if they're not everything you want or need today, just wait until tomorrow. Things are moving that fast.
3. If you don't know where to start, what questions to ask, or even how to imagine what's possible, you want to talk to someone who knows you well, knows your dreams and goals, and even knows your past mistakes so you can prevent them from happening again.

Why am I telling you this? I've "accidentally" built businesses my entire career. I started a couple of media companies and then some software companies, and I've done pretty well. All along the way, I've found ways to use computers, technology, marketing, copywriting, video, and content to build, grow, and scale businesses.

I'd love to say it was all planned out from the start, but I followed my gut most of the time. The Ai Revolution is the biggest opportunity of our lifetime–and any lifetime on the planet. What I'm saying is don't leave your success with the Ai opportunity to chance.

The biggest mistake made along the way was not getting a coach soon enough.

The best investments that I make every year include Strategic Coach with Dan Sullivan (who I have the good fortune of hosting a podcast with), Genius Network with Joe Polish (who I am now celebrating my 15th year with), and The Tony Robbins Organization (who I started coaching with way back in 1995).

And the best news of all is I've become very good friends with all of them, along with several other people, including Gay Hendricks, author of *The Big Leap* and *The Genius Zone* (who I also have the good fortune of hosting a podcast with).

The point is that surrounding myself with better coaches who are deeper thinkers than me has always given me the highest ROI out of any investment I've ever made. In fact, every single year I get a 10x return on my investment just from new business I received through the networks I'm a part of.

What does this have to do with you, and why does it matter?

Well, it's simple. Knowing what I know now and seeing the results that come quickly from implementing Ai in your business... The best thing you can do is find a coach who knows more than you do and who can help you grow.

Whether it's me and my organization or not isn't what's important, but I will tell you some ways that we can work together that provide the highest ROI in the shortest period.

The fastest and easiest thing to do is to hire a Fractional Ai Officer. That is someone who is already working with dozens of companies to implement Ai. They know all the best uses for Ai for a business like yours so you don't have to scratch your head to figure it out. They know how to ask you questions... questions you don't even know you should be asking.

Your Fractional Ai Officer will put tools and systems in place that will both make you and save you tens or hundreds of thousands of dollars right away.

Then, they can work with you to help you see opportunities for commercializing your IP to create recurring revenue and much bigger multiples for your business. A Fractional Ai Officer can help you achieve a big opportunity, overcome a big challenge, or allow you to spend more time in your superpower.

Your fractional Ai Officer can build tools that can do any or all of the following, including:

- Write a year's worth of professional copy by building a copywriting GPT based on your voice so that you don't have to train the Ai. They do it. And, you'll never again need to create a project, describe what you want, hire copywriters, wait, and then correct what they give you.
- Craft targeted messaging to attract your ideal customers that you can use right away.
- Create premium offers and pricing strategies so you can create new opportunities, new products, and new services that you can start selling in hours from now instead of days, weeks, or months.
- Develop your signature presentation or TED Talk to get in front of lots of high-value prospects tomorrow.
- Generate social media content that can be posted right now and have a system that allows you to do it again and again without having to wait for someone else.

- Summarize best practices and create SOPs in real-time, building systems that are repeatable without needing a human.
- Create emails–imagine if your email inbox had responses to all your messages already done, so all you have to do is review, tweak, and send.
- Create proposals based on your best "winners" that made you the most money.
- Create custom GPTs that augment or even replace high-cost labor, so your teams can focus on delivering even more value. It's not uncommon for us to save an organization $10,000, $25,000, or $75,000 with a single custom GPT.

The bottom line is that a talented Fractional Ai Officer can save you two to eight hours a week, tens of thousands of dollars in unnecessary expenses...and an immeasurable amount of frustration.

If you looked at just some of the playbooks that we've created, we built a massive library of reusable, repurposable tools that can be modified and applied in your business in a matter of hours. These are time-tested solutions based on all of the surveys I take when I speak to groups of business owners. They are the most important and useful Ai blueprints that virtually every business owner wants and needs, and they're already built. It's just plug-and-play.

So that's step one.

If you're not ready for the push-button convenience of a Fractional Ai Officer or you want to take a more hands-on approach, we have something called The Ai Accelerator. It is the fastest way to get your head around what's possible with Ai and how it can be used in your organization.

It's a hands-on, step-by-step, done-with-you experience where you walk away with an overview and understanding of not just how you can use Ai in your business. You'll also see how other people use it, giving you even more ideas. It's 100 percent practical and useful right now.

You can learn more by going to MikeKoenigs.com/GetAi.

You have IP. You have your secret sauce. You might not realize that all that wisdom and knowledge can be packaged into a product or service that could generate monthly recurring revenue. Your IP could be worth significantly more than the business you have right now.

If you want to apply The Trillionaire Ai Mindset™ and work with us to build and commercialize apps that can be used to automate challenging tasks in your business or even commercialize them, we have a development team that can rapidly build and create products in days or weeks instead of months or years. We've built functional, industry-specific chatbots in as little as a week that have been presented in front of real customers and investors and have been bootstrapped and monetized quickly. If you want to see an example of what's possible, make sure you check out our DigitalCafe.Ai sales acceleration tool at DigitalCafe.Ai.

If you want to learn more, book a session with us at MikeKoenigs.com/Talk.

Lastly, for the past seven years, The Superpower Accelerator team has bootstrapped and created brands, businesses, and products with complete marketing systems and sales tools in under a week. We've created over 100 businesses, brands, and products from scratch, including the entire business pitch, Keynote and PowerPoint presentations, sales and marketing videos, complete marketing systems, websites, landing pages, and everything you need to be able to go out and start selling the next day.

We've used the Superpower Accelerator system to:

- Reinvent America's 401(k) Coach, Charlie Epstein, as a stand-up comedian with his own one-man show, "The Yield of Dreams,"
- Create "The Lifestyle Investor" brand and offering for Justin Donald, who was a previous unknown and now has one of the best and largest brands in the investing and financial categories - and grew from $0 to $15 million in revenue in less than three years;
- Enable an up-and-coming entrepreneur, Coran Woodmass, to evolve into a new version of who he serves, how he works, and what he does; move from $7,000 to $75,000 offers; generate 26 leads in 48 hours; and close deals in a single call;
- Springboard interior designer Connie Wittich into an entirely new brand as the purveyor of "The DNA of Elevated Living," which now has her winning 90 percent of her business pitches and added an additional $6,000,000 in revenue in a single year;

- Recreate an eight-figure franchisor, Joey Osborne, as an advisor to other entrepreneurs hoping to sell their businesses (and save him from the boredom of retirement);
- Repackage and reposition Michael Chu's coaching program, increase the price to $50,000, and generate $1,200,000 in revenue in a single day;

And hundreds more.

If you're looking to reinvent yourself or your existing business, or if you've recently had an exit and you want to build a new business, The Superpower Accelerator is for you. I only wish I had a service like this after selling my last five businesses so I could have gotten re-started quickly.

You can find out more about the Superpower Accelerator at www.MikeKoenigs.com/go.

Now, I know you get lots of offers and opportunities and have loads of distractions in your life. This is not one of them. Ai is going to change your business THIS YEAR. I wrote this book so that you can capitalize on the amazing opportunities Ai gives you, right now.

To Your Ai Accelerated Future!

Mike

P.S. If you want to get immersed in more of my content and materials, go ahead and check out some of the examples, speeches, products, and tools at www.MikeKoenigs.com/AiBookBonus.

If you want to get started with the Ai Accelerator training, go to www.MikeKoenigs.com/GetAi.

If you want to talk to us about hiring a Fractional Ai Officer or talk to us about developing your own product to commercialize your IP, go to www.MikeKoenigs.com/Fractional.

If you want to learn more about the Superpower Accelerator process, go to www.MikeKoenigs.com/go.

Thanks for reading!

RESOURCES

Step 1: Get An Ai Blueprint for Your Business

No matter where you are in your Ai business journey, every business owner and entrepreneur asks me the same basic questions:

- How can I use Ai to get my time back?
- How exactly do I get started with Ai?
- What should I use it for?
- What can it do or not do?
- What programs and apps are best?
- How much time and money can I realistically save?
- Can Ai replace or augment my teams?
- Can I get rid of employees?
- And, how do I implement Ai smoothly without causing an internal mutiny?

Ever since Ai became mainstream, my team and I have shown thousands of business owners and founders how to use Ai to save hours of time each week, increase team productivity, automate annoying, difficult, or expensive tasks, and ultimately make more money without adding overhead.

Let's face it - employees can understandably be afraid of Ai replacing them. But implemented thoughtfully, Ai can make teams significantly more productive and profitable and free them from tedious tasks to focus on higher-value work.

Imagine... in less than half a day, you could get a plan and achieve "Ai Clarity" for your business:

- Learn exactly how Ai can help your specific business
- Discover the best applications based on your needs
- Walk away with a 90-day implementation plan guaranteed to drive revenue, productivity, and time savings

That's what our **Ai Accelerator Blueprint** delivers.

In a single discovery session, we'll audit your business, offers, website, challenges, and dreams and create a unique blueprint to get you where you want to go. We've already built solutions for nearly every B2B and B2C scenario, including healthcare, real estate, wealth management, investing, family offices, professional services, coaching, advisory, consulting, construction, software and SaaS, longevity, wireless and mobile, space, nutrition, and personal development.

After meeting 1:1 with an Ai Advisor, you'll get a customized 90-day plan outlining how to leverage Ai for a 3x-10x ROI within 100 days. I'm so confident in the results that if we can't identify an ROI, we'll refund your investment, no questions asked. With that in mind, we've never seen a business that doesn't get results quickly.

Next, you'll have a session with our Chief Ai Officer to deliver your plan, resources, and implementation recommendations. We'll describe what to do next so you hit the ground running and even prototype some solutions with you while we meet.

Businesses that don't take this approach are often confused and distracted by the non-stop parade of shiny objects and new Ai tools that are exciting but overwhelming.

- We focus on the outcome you want to achieve first.
- Then, we design workflows for you and your team.
- Then, we include proven, trusted, and flexible tools that produce results.
- With a plan of what to do first that provides the most value, time and money savings while creating income and equity for your business.

There is a lot you can Ai-ify in your business, but not everything needs to be. Not everything is going to move the needle. We're going to look for needle movers that will save you a tremendous amount of time and money while producing the revenue and productivity gains you want. Plus, we'll empower employees and create "Ai Innovation Mindsets."

I'll be 100% transparent with you. Once you get your blueprint, you're going to want to work with someone who can implement or train your teams to help you achieve your goals faster. We have a full "Done With You" and "Done For You" Fractional Ai team, which can get days or weeks of work done in hours.

Ready to get started? Visit www.MikeKoenigs.com/Start to schedule your discovery session and answer a few questions. Then we'll take it from there!

We're looking forward to showing you how Ai can transform your business.

Step 2: Hire a Fractional Ai Officer or Team

When I speak and present, a LOT of founders and entrepreneurs ask me, "I have total Ai overwhelm. What's the fastest way to implement Ai in my business, get my time back, automate annoying and repetitive tasks or just figure out how to get past the noise and endless "shiny Ai objects"?

The EASY "done with you" answer is to work with a Fractional Ai Officer. You don't have to find, hire, train, or test someone out. The best news is I've done all that hard work for you and saved you months of time and tens or hundreds of thousands of dollars.

And in just two hours, you can start saving time and money without the Ai Pain.

First off, you'll get all these questions answered:

- Where do I start?
- Is Ai right for my business?
- Is there any way to eliminate having to hire more people?
- Can I increase the productivity of my existing team by 2x-3x?
- How can I automate more processes?
- What technologies can help me scale?
- How do I systematize what's working while continuing to innovate?
- What should I be using Ai for and what shouldn't I?

That's why I created my Fractional Ai Officer program - to provide the Ai strategy and implementation help I wish I had when getting started.

Just this morning, I talked to my client Charlie Epstein, who we helped to launch his one-man comedy show called "Yield of Dreams," which makes retirement planning and wealth management funny and engaging. Well, Charlie is having great success with his outbound calling team, booking meetings with prospects, but he knew he could multiply his results even faster by adding Ai.

He asked if he could strategize with my Ai team on automating his processes.

Charlie saw that turning his already successful system into an automated Ai process could massively scale his growth. He's one of those "shoot for the moon" thinkers who always says yes to big, exciting ideas that have potential.

I suggested that an Ai system could analyze the thousands of calls made by his team and turn it into a training manual, best practices playbook, or even build an automated booking system.

That's just a taste of what a Fractional Ai Officer can do. In a few two-hour working sessions, we can:

- Show you how to automate nearly anything and everything in your business step-by-step, holding you or your team by the hand every step of the way
- Replace copywriters by building Ai content creators that capture your voice while generating endless high-converting copy for all your marketing

- Create systems that replace or augment customer service and support
- Develop your signature talk or keynote to go after your dream clients
- Review hundreds of hours of meetings, transcripts, and logs to create SOPs and document tacit knowledge and internal processes
- Build apps to automate tedious 20-30 hour weekly tasks down to minutes
- Strategize how Ai can help write books, course content, or anything that takes your time
- And so much more...

In fact, I've conducted thousands of surveys and interviews with business owners, entrepreneurs and founders from hundreds of different industries. Here are the "**Top 10 Most Valuable Ai Use Cases for Executives and Business Owners**":

1. Automating lead generation, prospecting, and outbound sales processes to save time and increase revenue.
2. Developing a personalized Ai assistant to handle emails, social media, proposals, and follow-ups to improve efficiency and find missed opportunities.
3. Enhancing customer experience through Ai-powered chatbots, personalized communication, and automated support while maintaining a human touch.
4. Creating Ai-driven content creation, including blog posts, videos, courses, and lead magnets, to scale thought leadership and attract qualified leads.

5. Integrating Ai into marketing strategies for targeted messaging, ad creation, and social media management to improve ROI and save time.
6. Automating repetitive tasks and processes within the business to reduce manual labor and increase productivity.
7. Utilizing Ai for data analysis, customer feedback, and market research to identify best practices, improve decision-making, and drive growth.
8. Developing proprietary Ai-powered software or tools to create equity in the business and generate additional revenue streams.
9. Implementing Ai for personalized customer onboarding, enrollment, and retention to scale the business and reduce churn.
10. Leveraging Ai for predictive analytics, trend forecasting, and risk assessment to stay ahead of the competition and make informed strategic decisions.

While the money you'll save and make is important, what I love most is seeing your mind expand to the art of the possible with Ai. You realize there are few limits. It's less about what Ai can't do but more about "Yes, I can use Ai to get that done!"

Here's the thing: employees can be understandably afraid of Ai replacing them. But when implemented thoughtfully, Ai can make teams significantly more productive and profitable, freeing them from tedious tasks to focus on higher-value work.

My Fractional Ai team has a simple process:

1. First, you **book a strategy session** where we will uncover your biggest business challenges and opportunities. We have dozens of use cases, case studies and examples to draw from. (This is the equivalent of the Step #1 Ai Blueprint)
2. Next, we **schedule FOUR working sessions** where we collaborate and actually build Ai solutions that make money, save time, and automate high-value tasks with you.
3. **Each session is a 1:1 strategic two-hour sprint** where you will get the most high-impact solutions with the least friction. They are FUN, and you walk away with finished solutions that work immediately.
4. Finally, after just four sessions, you'll walk away with **customized Ai solutions** along with the confidence and strategic clarity to apply Ai across your business.
5. And of course, **we can do this over and over again** - or find other ways to collaborate together including building custom Ai software, products, services or growing your brand, platform and impact.

Visit www.MikeKoenigs.com/Fractional to start your journey and get more done!

PS - If you've already done the Ai Blueprint process, we'll apply that investment to the Fractional Ai program!

DigitalCafe.Ai - It's Not Lead Gen. It's Leads Closed.

Welcome to the world of 3-second attention spans and fewer than 20 to get a prospect's attention, engage, get them to know, like, and trust you, and say, "I want and need what you have! Let's make a deal!"

You spend a fortune generating traffic and leads; chances are, your systems don't quickly, consistently, and competently follow up 24/7/365. Money loves speed, and time kills deals.

Introducing DigitalCafe.Ai, a relationship-building Ai that will take your hard-earned leads and make them feel like you're sitting down with them for a cup of coffee, listening to their needs, and responding to them with a personalized, useful, resourceful solution.

It's the perfect Ai team:

- An A+ marketer who gets attention and captures leads.
- A friendly salesperson who asks the most engaging questions.

- A data nerd who researches, enriches, qualifies your prospects, and predicts their behaviors.
- An engaging copywriter who follows up in your voice with stories that connect so your prospect feels seen, heard, and understood.
- And a delivery genius who makes sure every message gets read, heard, and watched minutes after first contact.

Your prospects get a hyper-personalized follow-up message, story, proposal, brochure, videos, audios, voicemail, email, and custom website that gives them a sense of hope, possibility, and vision to invest in your product or service. It creates beautiful magazine-quality PDF reports. It even sends real handwritten cards and letters right to their home!

DigitalCafe.Ai does hours or days of work that normally requires an EXPENSIVE team of specialists…in minutes. You get instant notifications of qualified prospects, so you or your team can take over the conversation or let Ai do the work for you. You see everything your prospect does in real time. It's the fastest, easiest automated way to get attention, engagement, and trust and close bigger deals faster.

Your prospect is blown away by the experience. Every deal closes faster with less work. No HR issues. No complaints. No excuses. No vacations. Always on, 24/7/365.

It's not about taking the human interaction out. It's filling the void where the human component falls on its face.

NOW you're probably asking: "Is it easy? Does it work? Will it work for me and my business?"

DigitalCafe.Ai is a done-for-you service that can be adapted to any B2B or B2C business, understand any language, anywhere in the world. It integrates with every CRM system and even connects to WhatsApp, which means 100% deliverability with no CAN-SPAM, SMS, text, or GDPR limitations!

Money loves speed, and time kills deals.

Visit www.DigitalCafe.Ai to see how it will work for you.

Get the Latest in Ai Training for You and Your Team!

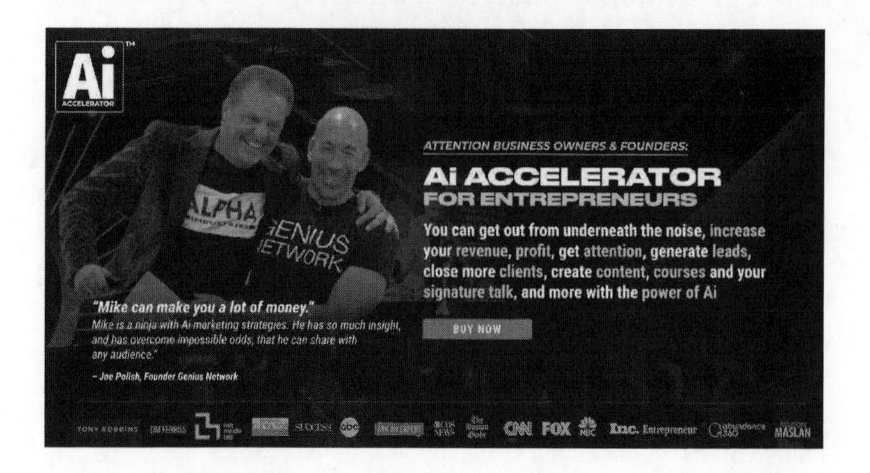

If you're not ready for the push-button convenience of a Fractional Ai Officer or you want to take a more hands-on approach, we have something called The Ai Accelerator, which is a live, quarterly, cohort-style, group training program. It's dedicated and focused entirely on founders, entrepreneurs, and business owners to help you use and apply Ai in your business. It gives you access to our huge library of step-by-step playbooks that allow you to "hit the ground running" using Ai in your business.

We meet weekly for 60 to 90 minutes. Every session is recorded and custom-made based on the needs of the people attending. You'll have an onboarding session where you can meet with one of my team members, who will get to know you and learn about your business and your needs and challenges.

Here's what we'll accomplish together:

- **Increase Revenue** - My team will help you create high-converting offers, presentations, and marketing campaigns using our proven Ai tools and systems. Most clients 3-10X their income.

- **Save Time** - Ai can automate tedious tasks like writing, research, data entry, and more that burn hours each day. We'll build customized solutions for your biggest time sucks.

- **Enhance Your Team** - I'll show you how to streamline everything from hiring and onboarding to creating SOPs. This lets your team focus on high-impact work.

- **Become an Ai Leader** - You'll get hands-on training, access to the latest Ai directory, and 18 step-by-step Ai Playbooks covering every aspect of scaling with Ai.

- This is a complete A-Z system designed specifically for entrepreneurs and business owners. You don't need any prior Ai or tech experience. We make it simple.

Here's what's included:

- 1:1 Onboarding Session
- 12 Weekly 90-minute Live Group Training Sessions
- Hot Seat Group Coaching During Each Session
- Private Community Access
- 18 Plug & Play Ai Playbooks
- Recordings & Transcripts Of Every Session
- Ai Tools Directory & Resources
- Bonuses Like Bestselling Books & Courses

I promise that after 90 days, you'll have fully integrated Ai to drive faster growth or your money back.

Let my team and I show you how to leverage this technology to accelerate your success.

Ready to 10X your business? Join the Ai Accelerator now!

www.MikeKoenigs.com/GetAi

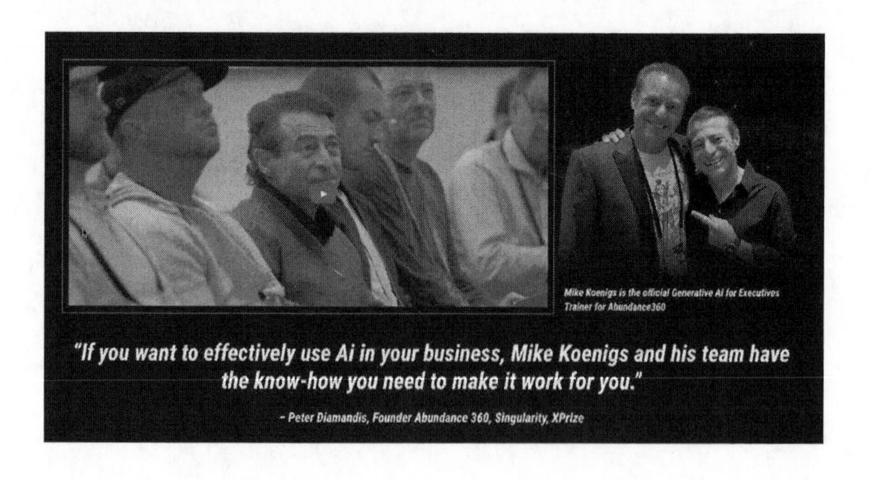

Mike Koenigs is the official Generative AI for Executives Trainer for Abundance360
"If you want to effectively use Ai in your business, Mike Koenigs and his team have the know-how you need to make it work for you."
- Peter Diamandis, Founder Abundance 360, Singularity, XPrize

Reinvent Yourself or Your Business in Just One Week

From the Desk of Mike Koenigs,

You might know me from teaching Ai Workshops for Tony Robbins, Peter Diamandis Abundance360, Dave Asprey's BioHacking Live, Joe Polish's Genius Network, MIT, YPO, EO or the work I've done with Dan Sullivan and Strategic Coach, Darren Hardy, JJ Virgin, BMW, Sony, 3M, General Mills, my podcast with Dan Sullivan, Gay Hendricks, or articles in Entrepreneur, Fast Company or Forbes. I know that's a bunch of name-dropping, but it'll make sense in a moment.

I've worked with thousands of entrepreneurs over the past 30 years, and here's what I've learned: You (and every entrepreneur and founder), at one time or another, face any or all of the following:

1. **You need an upgrade and probably want to find ways to use Ai to grow your business.** Your current business needs a reinvention - better offers, higher-ticket products, better customers, upgraded packaging, positioning, messaging, and systems to grow your business and increase your revenue. You've probably worked with

many people and organizations, but you're looking for a better, faster way to results.

2. **You're ready for Your Next Act and want to create or grow a strong personal brand.** You've recently exited or want to reinvent yourself. Still, finding a team that understands what you want and need and creates all the "stuff" to establish authority, pre-eminence, thought leadership, branding, messaging, and offers to get your next big thing off the ground quickly is hard, expensive, and time-consuming…

3. **You're stuck.** You've outgrown who you are, what you do, why you're doing it, and who you're doing it for. You want to do something new with more impact, fewer moving parts, high NET, and low overhead that's lifestyle compatible… but don't know what "it" is…and need a creative partner to turn vision into reality. You need someone to help you think bigger with the ability to make it real.

After 30+ years of building and selling five companies myself, I focus my attention on helping entrepreneurs create and launch:

"Your Next Act:
A Business You'll Love for the Rest of Your Life."

In just one week, my incredibly talented team and I collaborate with you 1:1 and create:

- A Unique "Category of One" **Brand or Product Offering**
- A Ready-to-Present **Offer** and Presentation
- Credibility and Thought Leadership Building **Content**
- Sales and Marketing **Sales Video** that Sells Products and Gets You Noticed
- Collateral and **Content** to Overcome Sales Objections
- Visibility-Enhancing **Articles**, in Entrepreneur, Forbes or Fast Company
- **Top 1% featured Podcast** and **promotion** to my audience of over 200,000
- A **Business Model** and Delivery System that's Easy to Deliver and Profitable
- Every step of the way, **we use Generative Ai and the latest cutting-edge tools**, tech and resources to rapidly create and iterate systems and software to speed up the process...
- I open my 30+ year **Database of Connections to** my relationships, vendors and even clients who can 10x your business...

Many of my clients say the connections and relationships I make through my network are as transformative and profitable as the work we do together.

What generally takes months and sometimes years happens in less than a week.

"Your Next Act" is a proven framework my team and I used to create and launch a new business six months ago with a client that **landed him a $35mm deal after spending just three days together**...

Two weeks after we created his new brand, he sent me this message...

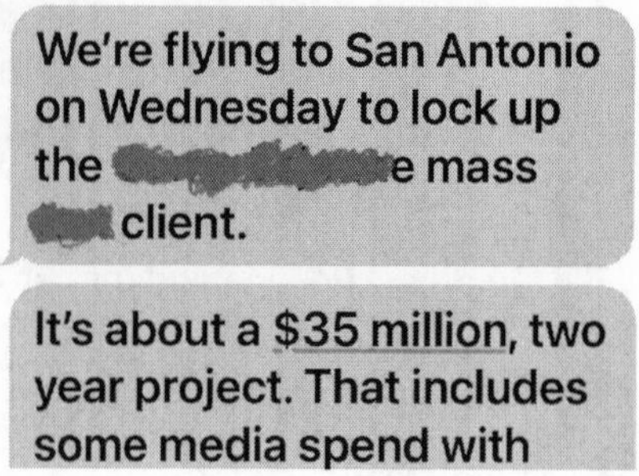

We're flying to San Antonio on Wednesday to lock up the [illegible]e mass [illegible] client.

It's about a $35 million, two year project. That includes some media spend with

Just before the annual Abundance 360 event, we worked with **Tim Nelson, MD, PhD from HeartWorks** on his packaging, positioning, messaging and presentation to raise money for their Nobel-winning, life-saving stem cell platform and to move towards commercialization. That presentation raised $500,000 in 15 minutes.

It's the same system we used to create **Justin Donald's brand and platform, "The Lifestyle Investor,"** that produced over 8-figures in less than three years...

Financial Advisor, Charlie Epstein launched "Yield of Dreams", a one-man comedy show that outperforms traditional marketing by 5:1, producing more revenue in 60 days than every other financial advisor who uses traditional methods in a year!

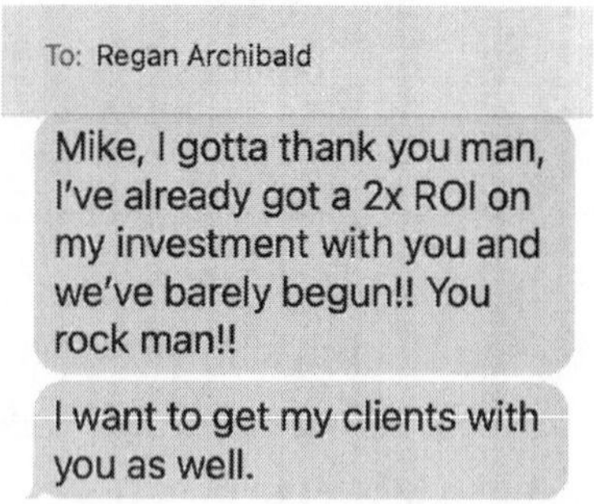

To: Regan Archibald

Mike, I gotta thank you man, I've already got a 2x ROI on my investment with you and we've barely begun!! You rock man!!

I want to get my clients with you as well.

The list goes on and on - It's the system my longevity advisor, "The Peptide Expert"

Regan Archibald, used to generate hundreds of thousands of dollars in new business from a single strategy in days…

Your Next Act works in any industry, for any business owner or entrepreneur, anywhere in the world: from software, real estate, healthcare, medical, biotech, financial services, wealth management, investing, professional services, legal, private equity, insurance, business coaching and advising, space, software, SaaS, construction and manufacturing.

Any industry that needs CUSTOMERS or CLIENTS and can benefit from better packaging, positioning, and messaging to raise awareness, create more engagement and generate more impact...

Meet Justin Donald. We met on a business trip to Fiji. I asked him what he did for a living. He said, "I'm a cash flow investor." I asked him what that meant, and after about half an hour, it finally made sense.

Justin had gone from having a regular job as a sales manager for Cutco knives with a personal net worth of under a million dollars (doing small investments) to increasing **his net worth an additional $10 million in less than 21 months and now over $100 million in less than four years**. And it's continued to grow. All before his 40th birthday. He had figured out how to find investments, de-risk, negotiate crazy terms, and finance deals in ways I had never heard of. I'm positive Justin will be a billionaire before his 50th birthday.

Back to meeting him the first time in Fiji… While we were speaking, I searched for him online and discovered Justin had **a ZERO** footprint; he **was invisible**. Like nothing - even social media. No website, brand, domain, or offer. I asked him if he had ever thought about writing a book, speaking, or teaching his system to the world. He said he'd love to but had **NO IDEA** how to begin.

What he *did* know was that he wanted to share his story of how anyone could achieve financial freedom like he and his wife, Jen did - while earning enough passive income to never have to work again.

I told him, "You're the Genius nobody has heard of, and you've met the right person at the right time to change that."

Justin enrolled in our " Superpower Accelerator Workshop Experience." We went to work and created a unique "Category of One" brand for Justin, which simply means he has no direct competition. Becoming a Category of One brand means Justin never has to deal with price-shoppers, tire-kickers just looking to compare offers, or losing potential clients to competitors.

Over three days, we launched "The Lifestyle Investor" and created $50,000 and $250,000 offers and marketing tools and resources to engage and enroll prospects. Over the next few months, we had his book written, launched a podcast, and we featured him in Entrepreneur and Forbes magazines to create awareness and elevate his authority, thought leadership and brand awareness.

The same day we crafted his offer, **I made just one intro to a business owner in my network... who became his first $250,000 client.** The following week, he used our sales system and enrolled another $250,000 client.

Less than eight months after we began working together, Justin made over a million dollars in revenue. Two weeks after his book was launched, it sold over 10,000 copies. It was an instant bestseller and sold many thousands more to achieve #1 in the Wall Street Journal, USA Today, and #8 ***overall*** on Amazon.

Here's proof:

THE WALL STREET JOURNAL.

Home World U.S. Politics Economy Business Tech Markets Opinion **Life & Arts** Real Estate

Bestselling Books Weeks Ended January 23

TITLE	AUTHOR/PUBLISHER	THIS WEEK	LAST WEEK
The Lifestyle Investor: The 10 Commandments of Cash Flow Investing for Passive Income and Financial Freedom	Justin Donald/Ethos Collective	1	New
Till Murder Do Us Part	James	2	New

Look inside

THE LIFESTYLE INVESTOR

THE 10 COMMANDMENTS OF CASH FLOW INVESTING FOR PASSIVE INCOME AND FINANCIAL FREEDOM

JUSTIN DONALD

Follow the Author

Justin Donald ✓ Following

The Lifestyle Investor: The 10 Commandments of Cash Flow Investing for Passive Income and Financial Freedom Kindle Edition

by Justin Donald (Author), Ryan Levesque (Foreword), Mike Koenigs (Foreword) | Format: Kindle Edition

82 ratings

#1 Best Seller in Financial Services

See all formats and editions

Kindle	Hardcover	Paperback
$0.99	$24.99	$14.09
Read with Our Free App	2 Used from $33.74 5 New from $24.99	2 Used from $20.24 5 New from $14.09

Create the Freedom & Lifestyle You've Always Dreamed About without a Job or Business

Let's face it. You want more—more money and freedom, less work, and a higher quality of life.

What if there were a simple, proven system to get you off the hamster wheel, create cash flow, and generate real wealth with little risk or complexity?

Bottom line... we created a new business from scratch with someone with no "footprint", generated over $1,000,000 in income which now exceeds $8,000,000 annually with massive margins, created massive connections, built a "strike force team" to handle the details, lots of buzz, pre-eminence, authority, and "super credibility" in the wealth-building category - one of the most competitive categories in the world.

"The Vision Day Workshop" isn't about writing books. It's not about "personal brands." Rather, we focus way beyond that on what's really important: We create the STRATEGY, MESSAGE, STORY, business MODEL and SYSTEM that attracts, inspires, and makes your ideal audience want you and your products. We package and position you and your business in a whole new way. IN A WEEK.

We also build and prototype products, software and ideas in days using Ai systems that leverate your IP and data to find hidden opportunities or commercialize in ways you might not have thought of.

"Your Next Act" is about **UPGRADING** your and your business **IDENTITY** so that the world knows "YOU are so valuable," and your "OFFER is so compelling" that:

- You can charge 3-10 times more than you're charging now,
- Industry Leaders, Influencers, and Ambassadors gladly recommend you to their communities,
- You create word-of-mouth buzz, awareness, and referrals

- You are recognized as being so unique & valuable - you can't be outsourced or replaced,
- No one can steal your product or service and make it their own,
- You transform lives for your clients on multiple levels, and people love you for it,
- You get to spend 90+% of your time doing what you love, with people you love to work with,
- You're positioned so you never have to work with idiots, jerks or fools again,
- Your life is fulfilling and fun! As my mentor Dan Sullivan says - the Four Freedoms of Time, Money, Purpose and Relationship

That's what The Superpower Accelerator does and what the Vision Day Workshop is all about. We turn dreams and visions into reality and we do it **QUICKLY.** We're the WHO that creates the HOW.

One of our "Category of One" that sets us far apart is how quickly we ACCELERATE our clients' progress and set them up for IMMEDIATE RESULTS. The truth is... *We get more done in 72 hours than most can in 6-18 months (or ever) because we implement and execute immediately.*

We do it in THREE DAYS ***with you***. **Without any homework on your part**. You show up and stay at my La Jolla condo across the street from the Pacific Ocean.

Justin Before: When we first met Justin was the "passive income genius" no one knew about. He was invisible to the world - no website, no email list, no social media, and no products or services to sell. His net worth was approaching 8 figures.

Justin - one week after we started working together: Justin had his new Superpower Accelerator mindset, market, and messaging right - resulting in 2 new clients paying him $250,000 each for his advice. (That's $500,000 in a Week!) And, he had clarity and an exact plan to move ahead, he knew his model for making money, his pitch, his offer and the most effective media to use to attract his perfect client.

Justin - 6 months later: Justin's Superpower Accelerator mindset made things happen fast. Within months he had his income model in place with a new website selling $500-$5,000 products and $50,000-$250,000 programs.

Justin - just 20 months after we worked together: Last year I was in Austin at Justin's $50,000 per year passive income mastermind. Almost 100 people were in the room. He told me the good news - **less than two years after we started working together, he's produced $7.5mm in yearly sales**.

At the same time, the media plan we designed and executed for him took off... resulting in his #1 bestselling book, *The Lifestyle Investor,* AND a top of charts podcast giving him a platform to reach anyone he wants to talk to, and articles in Forbes and Entrepreneur that called him the "Warren Buffet of Lifestyle Investing."

"Deciding to work with Mike and his team accelerated everything... Mike is a Superpower Accelerator."
—Justin Donald

READY TO BECOME A "CATEGORY OF ONE" IN RECORD TIME YOURSELF? HERE'S WHAT TO DO NEXT:

1. Go to www.MikeKoenigs.com/Go to schedule a brief Zoom conversation with me or my Director of Client Experience. If you know your KOLBE, you're definitely an 8, 9, or 10 QuickStart because ***you know you want Your Next Act right now.***
2. We'll ask you a few questions to get to know you and your business better and discuss how we can help you create Your Next Act, reach more, better-fit clients, elevate your brand and visibility, increase or improve the size of your transactions and make sure we are confident we can get you the amazing results the Superpower Accelerator is known for.
3. If we decide we're a mutual fit, we'll schedule your 3-day 1:1 workshop and start the onboarding process. No pressure. No gimmicks.

The industry or business category doesn't matter because, at the end of the day, there's only one real thing that matters for any business... A great offer, a great pitch, and **CUSTOMERS**.

Now, if working together on Your Next Act isn't interesting or relevant to you right now, no problem.

Enjoy this book, my podcasts and other content.

But if you know in your heart that you need help, now is the time to work with a team that can take you and your business to the next level as a creative, visionary partner and collaborator.

Your Superpower Accelerator is here.

Mike Koenigs

PODCASTS AND BOOKS

Podcasts

I produce two weekly podcasts designed to grow your business and improve your mindset.

CAPABILITY AMPLIFIER with Dan Sullivan, founder of Strategic Coach

The "Capability Amplifier" podcast is about sharing useful, intellectual shortcuts, with the smartest man in business, Dan Sullivan, founder of Strategic Coach. Most episodes are typically only Dan and me, but we occasionally interview fascinating guests like Suzy Batiz (founder of Poo Pourri), investor Steve Jurvetson, Shari Salata, Gino Wickman, Jason Flom, Yakov Smirnoff, Adam Conover and other fascinating guests. Subscribe at www.CapabilityAmplifier.com

RECENT + UPCOMING EPISODES:

- HOW TO CREATE A MAINSTREAM MIRACLE MOVEMENT WITH HAL ELROD
- THE ART OF SLOW THINKING WITH DEREK SIVERS
- SHERI SALATA - MEET OPRAH'S PRODUCER OF 20+ YEARS
- BIOHACK YOUR BRAIN, BODY AND BUSINESS WITH DAVE ASPREY
- ROBO TAXIS AND AUTONOMOUS VEHICLES WITH STEVE JURVETSON
- SH*T TALKING WITH SUZY BATIZ, FOUNDER OF POO-POURRI
- GET SMART WITH ADAM CONOVER OF "ADAM RUINS EVERYTHING"

THE BIG LEAP - with Gay Hendricks

I host a second podcast, "The Big Leap," with Gay Hendricks, a multiple New York Times bestselling author and a coaches' coach. The focus is on the decisions in life that change everything and the "Upper Limits" challenge every high performer deals with. The difference between stagnation and success lies in the decisions you make in the moments that matter.

This podcast is about THOSE turning points—the single decisions in life and business that changed everything. Subscribe at www.BigLeapPodcast.com

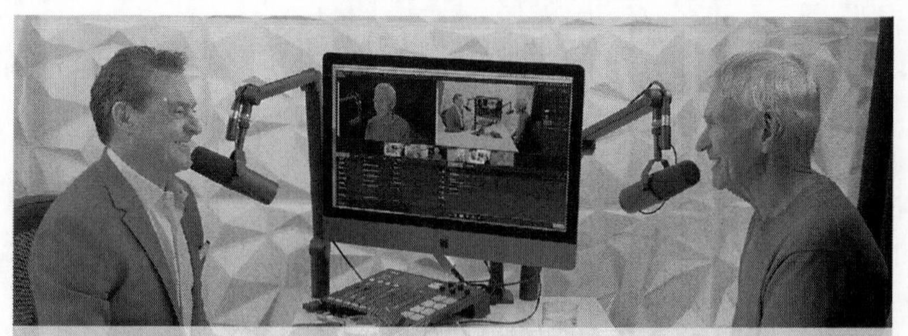

RECENT + UPCOMING EPISODES:

- THE EVOLUTION OF A RENAISSANCE MAN - STEVEN SASHEN, CREATOR OF XERO SHOES
- KEVIN NEALON - HIS BIG LEAPS INTO COMEDY AND ART
- WHY YOU SHOULD NEVER STOP TRYING WITH KIRSTEN VANGSNESS
- ATTAINING, ATONING AND ATTUNING WITH CHIP CONLEY
- BILL MOSES' EPIC JOURNEY WITH KEVITA AND FLYING EMBERS
- THE INTERSECTION OF COMEDY + TRANSFORMATION WITH KYLE CEASE
- THREE WAYS TO CREATE A BETTER FUTURE WITH JIM SELMAN

Books

Find out more at www.MikeKoenigs.com/NextAct

THE 6 GROWTH ACCELERATORS FOR CREATING A BUSINESS YOU'LL LOVE FOR THE REST OF YOUR LIFE

A Step-by-Step Guide to Reinventing You and Your Business

You and every entrepreneur, at one time or another in your career, face any or all of the following:

- You're stuck. You've outgrown who you are, what you do, why you're doing it, and who you're doing it for. You want to do something new that has more impact and joy...but don't know what it is..
- You need a reinvention. You're ok with your current business but need a total upgrade–better offers, higher-ticket products, and better customers.
- You're ready for Your Next Act. You've recently exited, but finding a team to create all the "stuff" to get it off the ground quickly is hard, expensive, and time-consuming...
- The path to higher revenue, more impact, and greater fulfillment is to create a category-of-one brand where the ideal customers and clients come to you already sold on your products and services. This short audiobook by business expert and serial entrepreneur Mike Koenigs will help you:
- Develop the right mindset of non-negotiable values to reimagine your business
- Target the ideal market who you can effectively serve, i.e.; who do you want to be a hero to?

- Design a profitable business model to deliver a brand promise, transformation, and simplify delivery
- Pinpoint the message that resonates with your perfect prospects, makes them raise their hands, and buy quickly
- Choose the proper media to get in front of your audience and drive them to buy now
- Amplify your success with a variety of multipliers that attract and close your market

Your Next Act works in virtually every industry for virtually every business owner or entrepreneur anywhere in the world: including funded startups, financial services, wealth management, investing, professional services, legal, private equity, insurance, business coaching and advising, space, software, Saas, construction, manufacturing, real estate, and healthcare.

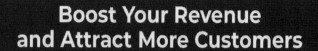

If you want more customers, you need this book!

THE ULTIMATE GUIDE TO GROWING YOUR BUSINESS WITH ZERO FUNNELS, ZERO ADS AND ZERO COSTS

Serial entrepreneur, business expert, and best-selling author Mike Koenigs shows you the only marketing system you need to fill your pipeline with qualified leads. Generate six- and even seven-figures in revenue, fast — without a complicated funnel, a large team, or tons of moving parts.

This "secret" system is the Referral Party process, and it has generated literally millions of dollars for Mike and his clients.

If you're looking for a simple way to generate more leads and book more sales, jump into this step-by-step guide and learn:

- WHY marketing has gotten too complicated and costly (and how Referral Parties provide an optimal alternative)
- WHO to partner with to ensure you both end up with valuable (and qualified), "right-fit" referrals
- WHAT to say to your referrals to get them to book immediately
- HOW to brief your referral partner so they intuitively know who in their network is the perfect lead for you
- MUST-HAVE TECHNOLOGY to keep the process (and dollars) flowing

You'll get word-for-word scripts, swipe-and-change templates, and tons of case studies and examples to get you started.

Use this guide to shortcut the steps most businesses are going through to find their perfect clients with Referral Parties.

THE SHORTCUT SERIES
Punch The Elephant
HOW TO SELL ANYTHING TO ANYONE AND OVERCOME ANY OBJECTION... EVEN IF YOU'RE BAD AT SALES
MIKE KOENIGS
A Superpower Accelerator Book

If you want to punch up your sales game or think you hate selling, this book is for you Serial entrepreneur, business expert, and best-selling author Mike Koenigs has spent decades studying human psychology, motivation, business, and language, in order to crack the code on sales.

The result: A sure-fire way to get people to not just buy from you, but want to buy from you (there's a big difference!).

The Superpower Accelerator Lightning Close is so straightforward and simple, it will outperform any other "process," "framework," or "secret" being touted by the so-called gurus and experts.

It's been used by thousands of people in hundreds of different industries to "punch the elephant" and make the sale (one client closed a deal worth $35M within days of learning this method!)

Mike Koenigs is a serial entrepreneur with five exits, judge on Entrepreneur.com's "Elevator Pitch" TV show, 18x bestselling author, contributor and columnist for Entrepreneur, Fast Company, and Forbes magazines. He co-hosts two podcasts, "Capability Amplifier" with Strategic Coach's Dan Sullivan and "The Big Leap" with NYT Best-Selling Author, Gay Hendricks.

He's consulted and advised major brands, including Sony, BMW, General Mills, 3M and celebrity clients, including Tony Robbins, Paula Abdul, Richard Dreyfuss, Dave Asprey, John Assaraf, Brian Tracy, Peter Diamandis, Daniel Amen, and Darren Hardy.

MEET MIKE KOENIGS

What's "Your Next Act?" Imagine creating and launching your next business that you'll love for the rest of your life, a strong personal brand that multiplies the value of everything you do, attracts high-value customers, generates better prospects, and closes deals faster...in a week?

Mike Koenigs is a serial entrepreneur with five successful exits and experience as a judge on Entrepreneur.com's "Elevator Pitch" TV show, Mike has the expertise to help founders create "Your Next Act," a business they'lIl love for the rest of your life. He collaborates with his clients to develop brands, products, pitches, offers, marketing content, and launches, all in just one week.

Mike is dedicated to helping founders create businesses that are high net, low overhead, high impact, and low stress, allowing them to spend more time in their superpowers. He has consulted with major brands, including Sony and BMW. He has advised high-profile clients, including Tony Robbins, Paula Abdul, Richard Dreyfuss, Dave Asprey, John Assaraf, Brian Tracy, Peter Diamandis, Daniel Amen, and Darren Hardy.

BOOK MIKE KOENIGS TO SPEAK

to Make Your Event Inspirational, Motivational, Highly Entertaining, and Unforgettable!

Peter Diamandis calls Mike Koenigs "*An Arsonist of The Mind.*" **Tony Robbins** *says: "Mike is an extraordinary man. He's brought me insights on how to reach people on the Internet that are so valuable. This is a man you should deal with. Take advantage of what he has to offer."*

Welcome to a journey of real-world, interactive, practical, tactical Ai case studies and mind-expanding live hotseats to show you how to "think in Ai" and how you can use the latest

Ai tools in your business and personal life. By the time this presentation is finished, you'll know how to save days or even weeks and adopt the most effective tools to create content that generally takes weeks to produce in hours, follow up with prospects, build marketing plans, write sales copy, books, produce sales systems, increase your revenue, and augment your teams and amplify your personal and business capabilities and creativity without being a technical whiz.

Mike will share some of his top resources and systems he's presented to Tony Robbins Platinum "Lions" mastermind group, Peter Diamandis' Abundance 360 Patron members, YPO, MIT's Media Lab, and even had the chance to share with the late 101-year-old Norman Lear about using Ai effectively (and profitably!)

Ai is the future of business; most experts agree "Your job or business won't be replaced by Ai. Someone who uses it will." Every business needs an Ai specialist, and you'll walk away understanding how to be your own or how to bring someone on your team up to speed!

Download Mike's current speaker and media kit at www.MikeKoenigs.com/MediaKit

Want to make your next event unforgettable? Book Mike as your keynote speaker. Head over to www.MikeKoenigs.com/Speaking or give them a call at +1 (858) 412-0858.

Take advantage of this opportunity to learn from the best!